Lifting my Nos from the Grind

Farming around the World

John Cherringtor

Northwood Books
London EC1V 7QA

LIFTING MY NOSE FROM
THE GRINDSTONE

Published 1981

ISBN 7198 2548 2

A 'Big Farm Management' book.

The photographs appearing on pages 60, 73 and 74 are reproduced by courtesy of *Farmers' Weekly*.

Typeset in Great Britain at The Grange Press, Southwick, Sussex. Printed at Anchor Press and bound at William Brendon Ltd, both of Tiptree, Essex.

Contents

farmers to roam afield will certainly be restricted. No doubt the retired and commuting workers will take over the burden of local government and the rest. The commuter with his five-day week, reducing I am certain to four, will fill the gap. The farmer on seven days will have willy-nilly to apply himself to his task continuously.

So I am fortunate in the period in which I have farmed and that I was able to afford the time spent out of my primary job. Afford is the right word. I have always been a freelance and freelances don't have pension schemes and employers with sick benefits. I have known freelances in broadcasting and journalism sick with worry that their producer or editor is going to change his mind or that they themselves could go sick and when recovered find they have been forgotten.

Although journalism is not vital to me, I have experienced this trauma with the best part of a year in and out of hospital never knowing if I would get back again. I knew that my basic farming was under the eye of my family and friends and in good shape but I certainly worried about the other. Unnecessary perhaps, but money isn't everything – interest is.

Why, you might ask, did I not go in for public work? I did, mainly in the NFU, but largely because I was driven by self-interest. Once I had obtained security of tenure the urgency went out of it. But what about the wider field, doing good for mankind as a whole? As a later chapter explains I did try public work in a political sense but failed to make my mark and was too impatient to try again. I can claim to have all the liberal, even socialist motives but have not the will to push them. The truth is that my convictions have not been compelling enough for me to sacrifice my inclinations on their behalf.

Why write this book? Just that I like writing, my publisher will buy it, and a large number of readers of my first effort, *On the Smell of an Oily Rag,* told me they wanted to know more of what I saw on my travels, with in-depth accounts of politics and the like, and even more about farming and the Common Market. I kept my first book concise as I didn't want the reader to get bogged down in detailed descriptive writing where the thread of the story could be lost.

The present book is based on my thoughts and experiences, mainly off my farm, over the last 30 years. For the last 20 or so I have been privileged to investigate various aspects of farming, farming politics and even general economics in Britain, Europe and around the world. Anyone can do this, of course, if he has enough money to buy the tickets. My good luck was that I was not only paid for most of this but that my findings were published. Don't assume from this that this book is just a collection dug

LIFTING MY NOSE FROM THE GRINDSTONE

Lifting my Nose from the Grindstone

Farming around the World

John Cherrington

Northwood Books
London EC1V 7QA

Published 1981

ISBN 7198 2548 2

A 'Big Farm Management' book.

The photographs appearing on pages 60, 73 and 74 are reproduced by courtesy of *Farmers' Weekly*.

Typeset in Great Britain at The Grange Press, Southwick, Sussex. Printed at Anchor Press and bound at William Brendon Ltd, both of Tiptree, Essex.

Contents

Preface

All my life I have had two jobs, sometimes several, at a time. Farming has always been my basic support and source of income but my peripheral occupations while only earning me a modest competence have afforded me the greatest interest and diversion, the latter essential for successful farming.

A farm, certainly a large farm, is rather like a massive steamer crawling over the seas on a preordained course under automatic control. Once it is going, its course is best not interfered with unless an emergency arises. All that is required is that a good watch be set and the Captain or boss keeps an experienced eye on things and knows where he is supposed to be going.

British farming is not, of course, as predictable as say plantation farming for sugar in the Tropics, but my experience is that once it is going well, the rotations set and each man knows what he is doing, there is nothing left for the boss to do. Except to be available in times of trouble with the ability to meet difficulties half way.

I am far from being the first to find this out. British farmers have been blessed with good labour for so long that they have abounded in local politics, the magistracy, sport and so on. With the departure of much of the squirearchy they have become the leaders of rural life because generally they are the only ones left with the time to spare. But this will not be for much longer.

The trend in the EEC is towards the family farm, where the farmer generally does the work. The divisive effects of the Code Napoléon on the Continent fragmented farming even more effectively than CTT promises do in this country. In Europe family farmers are efficient and highly competitive. They already exist in large measure here in the dairy districts and the proportion will spread. In consequence the opportunities for such farmers to roam afield will certainly be restricted. No doubt the retired and commuting workers will take over the burden of local government and the rest. The commuter with his five-day week, reducing I am certain to four, will fill the gap. The farmer on seven days will have willy-nilly to apply himself to his task continuously.

So I am fortunate in the period in which I have farmed and that I was able to afford the time spent out of my primary job. Afford is the right word. I have always been a freelance and freelances don't have pension schemes and employers with sick benefits. I have known freelances in broadcasting and journalism sick with worry that their producer or editor is going to change his mind or that they themselves could go sick and when recovered find they have been forgotten.

Although journalism is not vital to me, I have experienced this trauma with the best part of a year in and out of hospital never knowing if I would get back again. I knew that my basic farming was under the eye of my family and friends and in good shape but I certainly worried about the other. Unnecessary perhaps, but money isn't everything – interest is.

Why, you might ask, did I not go in for public work? I did, mainly in the NFU, but largely because I was driven by self-interest. Once I had obtained security of tenure the urgency went out of it. But what about the wider field, doing good for mankind as a whole? As a later chapter explains I did try public work in a political sense but failed to make my mark and was too impatient to try again. I can claim to have all the liberal, even socialist motives but have not the will to push them. The truth is that my convictions have not been compelling enough for me to sacrifice my inclinations on their behalf.

Why write this book? Just that I like writing, my publisher will buy it, and a large number of readers of my first effort, *On the Smell of an Oily Rag,* told me they wanted to know more of what I saw on my travels, with in-depth accounts of politics and the like, and even more about farming and the Common Market. I kept my first book concise as I didn't want the reader to get bogged down in detailed descriptive writing where the thread of the story could be lost.

The present book is based on my thoughts and experiences, mainly off my farm, over the last 30 years. For the last 20 or so I have been privileged to investigate various aspects of farming, farming politics and even general economics in Britain, Europe and around the world. Anyone can do this, of course, if he has enough money to buy the tickets. My good luck was that I was not only paid for most of this but that my findings were published. Don't assume from this that this book is just a collection dug out of the files, though these and my notebooks are the basis of what follows, often rewritten with hindsight.

So I should like here to thank the BBC, *The Financial Times, Farmers Weekly* and *Farmer and Stockbreeder,* who were the principal supporters of my activities. They have helped me attain the heights of any writer's ambition. I have always liked grinding axes but few of us are fortunate enough to be paid to do it.

TANGLEY
JUNE 1981

JOHN CHERRINGTON

Water is always a problem in Western Australia.

PART 1: AUSTRALASIA

1. A Town or Two Like 'Alice'

Lake Grace in Western Australia is a township at the southern end of the wheat belt. Its main feature is the lake, a wide expanse of solid salt stretching as far as the eye can see in the haze of a summer's day. Or at least until the mirage appears, an indistinct line of non-existent trees surrounding a non-existent blue lagoon. For that is what it looked like when I was trying to speak 'a piece to camera' when making a film on farming there. The background – that is, the mirage, which the producer was trying to incorporate into the scene – kept dissolving, as did the salt beneath my feet. The surroundings were hardly more salubrious. A dull olive-coloured scrub, mallee, a sort of dwarf eucalyptus and, where the land had been cleared, the khaki stubbles and pastures of an Australian summer.

The township, little more than two or three stores and a hotel with a few houses, is the centre for an area of large, 2,000 to 3,000 acre farms in what would be a 12 to 15 in rainfall belt. The farms had to be so extensive because the risks of drought in a marginal area would make smaller ones completely unviable. Even so, most of these farms employed no hired labour at all. The farmer, his wife, and his family if he had one, were the sole workers.

These farmers were mostly survivors of a post-war settlement scheme. Some of them had succeeded quite well, I was told. They had established their farms, and built a club and a bowling green. In the hotel bar that evening they seemed to be quite content with their lot. But what, I asked one of them, about their wives? How were they enjoying the isolation, the dust and the flies?

'Fine', said one of them. 'Did they never complain?' I asked. 'Well, some of them began to winge a bit, but we give them two afternoons a week on the bowling green and they are good now.' Winge is a typical Australian term for whining, often applied to Englishmen. 'Wingeing Pom' is a term of abuse, something no male Australian would be guilty of. In truth, Australian farmers have so many difficulties to contend with that any who winged would soon give up the ghost. For the whole continent makes a very harsh farming environment. It is subject to drought, except for parts of Queensland and around the North West. Even here the rainfall is monsoonal and thus seasonal. For the rest of the year conditions are very arid. There is none of the dense tropic growth found in the East Indies a few hundred miles to the north.

I have never believed that Australia remained unexploited until the first convicts were landed in Botany Bay because of any lack of enterprise by the Dutch and others who had been going to the East Indies since the 16th century. They and the Malays, their predecessors, had obviously seen and even landed in Australia. But not liking what they had seen, had up anchored and sailed away again. After all, a country which is burnt brown from October to May and in addition had a hostile population when any could be found had few attractions.

The shortage and irregularity of moisture is compounded by the threat of salt. No one knows exactly where the salt comes from, but there is a theory that the rainfall contains traces which over millions of years gradually impregnate the subsoil. Lake Grace is only one of many such salt lakes in Western Australia, and they are found elsewhere as well. The lakes are formed where the winter rains have run off on top of or below the soil. They are already heavily saturated with salt and with the evaporation in summer the solution eventually becomes completely dehydrated.

These lakes are the worst examples, but all over Western Australia one can see the increasing salination of the farming land. This is said to be due to the clearing of trees and scrub. According to the latest theory, before the clearance the rainfall was either used up by the trees or penetrated the clay subsoil by way of the roots of the vegetation. After clearance there was nothing to hold the moisture so it began to seep down the slopes, and was increasingly saturated by the salt in the soil as it reached the lower levels. There it either formed lakes or carried on in streams which were no more than saline solutions. A saline stream or lake can be identified by the crystalline clarity of the water. Sweet water is usually very muddy.

These saline areas are spreading dangerously wide, killing all vegetation of any economic value, particularly in Western Australia. I met farmers there who had lost up to a third of their farms in consequence and the salt is still spreading. This is particularly true of parts of the wheat belt where farmers are becoming very alarmed. The response of the Government scientific authorities appears to be that as the trouble was caused by clearing the trees, the obvious cure would be to replant. The effect of this advice on farmers who have spent their lives cutting their farms out of the same trees is quite predictable. There must be another way, they say.

One method is to try and seal the water flow across the slopes by cutting channels on the contour, so preventing the accumulations at the lower level. During 1980 alone some 800 kilometres of channels have been made and the scheme is gathering strength. There is a real desperation that unless they can do something effective, much of the wheat belt of Western Australia could eventually return to desert.

Western Australia is a particular interest of mine. During the 1960's very large areas of land were sold to farmers at extremely cheap rates – from 50p to £1 an acre. The land was completely untouched and much of it was in the Esperance area some 400 miles south-east of Perth. The sand plain country carried very little scrub, was in an area of good rainfall and recent research had shown that the addition of certain trace elements to the superphosphate of which the land was starved could make the land grow good pasture. There was a land boom reminiscent of the settling of America, and all sorts of farmers, including some from Britain, found their way there.

The land was all the enthusiasts claimed, but did need considerable capital to develop. A friend of mine, Denis Marshal, took up a block in 1958, cleared much of it and slowly increased the stock. But he was limited by lack of capital. Every acre cleared needed seed and fertiliser. Every block needed sheep or cattle. Fences don't grow of themselves. He built a barn and he and his wife and family lived in this for the next 15 years. Several times he worked out plans for a house, but before he could give the order to the builders, some accident of markets or the weather reduced his resources, and he had to cancel it.

He showed me his shower arrangements once. A bucket hung from the roof which he could tip into an old colander. His water collection for household supplies was limited to the roof of his barn. He had not yet found a spot where he could sink a bore to get water even unsalty enough for washing in, let alone cooking and drinking. On one occasion I met him he was hauling water from Esperance, 30 miles away. For his stock he relied on dams. Dams are conspicuous all over Australia. They collect the surface water even on almost flat country, then it is either pumped out for the stock or they water inside it. Being open to the sun they suffer from evaporation in the summer but they are the only source of water. They are usually very muddy but the water is sweet.

If you travel in Australia during the summer you will see sheep and cattle too grazing what looks to be little more than dust and a few stalks. The animals look well. They are living on what the Australians call summer feed, the seeds of clover and other legumes and the remains of the previous season's pasture. The main ingredient of pasture is subterranean clover, an annual Mediterranean plant that produces a seed which falls off when ripe and mixes with the surface dust. It is covered by a sort of hairy case which makes it easy to get into the soil. The animals don't eat them all so there is always a surplus left to germinate the next time it rains.

If you ask an Australian to show you his summer feed he will pick up a handful of earth and sift out the seeds. There are two problems. If there should be unseasonable rain at any time between November and April, it will cause the seeds to germinate. Then, should it get dry again, the seeds will die before they have a chance to make any real growth. So a premature greening of the pastures is a matter for great anxiety. Sub clover developed extremely well in the Esperance area, but then came the second problem. The varieties used produced a hormone in the West Australian conditions which caused the ewes to become infertile. This is being overcome, but is being succeeded by a bacterial wilt which is reducing the proportion of clover in the sward.

Over the years I have seen a continual dashing of Australian farmers' hopes through drought, disease and bad markets, which would have had the European farmers screaming for help on every side. Yet the Australians appear to be able to face these hazards and the hardships of their lives without undue worry and until very recently no Government help at all. Even now they are only getting a little help when a drought causes a major disaster.

The Government has given some very expensive help with irrigation. The Murray River system has been brought almost to the limit of irrigation – some would say pushed beyond it. This again is the result of salinity. Surplus water pumped out for irrigation seeps back into the river through the soil and in its travels picks up salt from the subsoil. This means that the nearer the mouth the higher the salinity. This is leading to acrimonious disputes and demands to limit irrigation.

The western district of Victoria comprises some of the best land in the whole country. The land is quite good, there is ample sweet water and a

Salt damage after clearance, W.A.

Western Australia: after 20 years the Marshalls still have not been able to build a house.

Fence drifted over by wind erosion through over cropping, Victoria.

South Australia: pasture.

fairly mild climate. My host on one farm told me that after the first £100,000 he was only able to keep 13 shillings in the £. He had a beautiful farm and his sons and daughters were prominent in the polo-playing aristocracy. But they had one characteristic not found among the British landowning élite – every man's hands were battered by years of hard work. They were good practical men and so they had to be because the wages they paid to their workers were so bad it was essential that they led the work. No man who was any good would stay and work in those conditions. The moral of this is that, if you want to become established in Australian farming, the only certain road to the top is to compromise the offspring of a squatter in the western districts of Victoria. This, I might say, is the only place I would have even considered. But alas I was too old when I found this out.

The Darling Downs in southern Queensland form one of the best areas of good land in Australia. The land is a black cotton soil of considerable natural fertility and is absolutely dead flat. A friend of mine, a very good practical farmer, better than the average in Australia, emigrated there from Hampshire. He assimilated well and bought a very good farm and farmed it well. He was able to store water in the backwater of a river which at the time I saw it was no more than a dribble between very high banks. His crops were cotton, barley, sorghum and soya beans. When I saw him last he had built a new house, increased his acreage to a thousand and was employing a man.

Life had not been easy though. A flood had reached the foundations of his new house, causing them to twist, and when I stayed there, no doors would close. Sometimes there was enough rainfall for him to fill his backwater and so irrigate. On other occasions he had to leave off cropping because there was no water. When things were good it was fine, but in the Australian climate nothing is very good for ever. If he had a good run he thought he was made, but then flood or drought upset him again. In 1981 I was going up to see him and knew that he had had a bad drought which might prevent him from growing a summer crop. In Sydney I read that there were floods 5 m deep in his local town. All the phones were out of order, so I did not manage to phone him. I hadn't the heart to call unannounced.

In western New South Wales I stayed on an old-established station. Here again the wisdom of the older settlers was in evidence. It was on the only permanent river in those parts and irrigation was possible. The guest bathroom had gold-plated taps. The farm ran to 70,000 acres and some was share-cropped for wheat. There was a stud of prize cattle and some

20,000 sheep. The farm was supported, I thought, by about 10,000 acres of wheat, of which the owner took 30 per cent and for which he paid for the fertiliser. His net for that was about £5 per acre, or £50,000, paid him by the Wheat Board, which handles all sales. A major problem had been kangaroos which had invaded the property in the last drought. Some 60,000 had had to be shot! Kangaroos are a great pest in some areas and have been made worse by the provision of drought-proof water supplies. They just come in and drink from the troughs.

Droughts are not quite the disaster they used to be. Since the provision of road transport stock can be moved hundreds of miles to where there is feed, and under drought relief the Government pays some of the costs. A more traditional scheme is to make use of the stock routes. These tracks, up to 100 yd wide, are often carrying more feed than the land behind the fences because most direct transport is by lorry. In one area of New South Wales I passed about a dozen huge flocks of sheep being minded along the routes. They are not supposed to stay too long in any one spot, but I was told some flock owners tried to overstay their welcome and take all the feed and, more serious, the water supplies. Landowners through whose properties they pass are supposed to let them in to water and to use their shearing sheds and yards.

So far I have been talking about the land which can be farmed for temperate or sub-tropical products, and of course meat and wool. There is dairying, particularly in Victoria, Queensland and West Australia, where there is a chance of adequate rainfall. But Australian dairying I thought was hard and insecure when compared with New Zealand and Europe. Cows prefer lush wet herbage and while these can be provided through irrigation this is scarce and expensive in most parts of Australia.

No land remains unexploited. Pastoral farming of sheep and cattle means just what it says The stock lives on the country as best it can at stocking rates which sound absurdly low to Europeans. From 10 to 30 acres to keep a sheep and anything up to 100 acres to keep a cow and calf!

About 300 miles north of Adelaide I spent a day on a sheep station some 50 miles off the main road to Alice Springs. The road to it, no more than a track, was hard to follow but for the line of empty beer bottles which seemed to be touching each other all along the way. For some reason there has never been any deposit on beer bottles so there is nothing to do but throw them away. They have now been joined by empty cans. At every gate there was a pile of this debris where the travellers, musterers or shearers had refreshed themselves before pushing on.

Station owners used to frown on those bringing drink to the establishments. I am sure that any one lost would be able to find his way to safety by following them.

Incidentally, that is bad advice unless you have a car and plenty of petrol and water. If this breaks down the only thing to do is camp by the car and wait for help. If you have been sensible and advised your destination of an expected time of arrival all you have to do is sit by your car, in the shade if possible, and wait for help to arrive. Every year the odd traveller fails to obey this rule, starts to walk, and in the great heat dehydrates and dies. Even if you don't have water in a can you always have the radiator to fall back on. Some of these disasters occur within the bounds of what could be called civilisation, so sparse is the population. The vegetation on the route was of salt and blue bush on which the sheep and cattle browsed. I saw none at all, only kangaroos and a few emus. To the north of the track were the Flinders Ranges, low rocky hills, and in between was a line of bigger trees marking a creek or watercourse which might or might not hold water. The land was very gently rolling.

This particular place was stocked with about one sheep to ten acres, largely a stock of Merino wethers kept entirely for their wool, which here grew some of the best in Australia. The work on the station was mainly fencing, repairing the windmills which pumped water, and killing kangaroos and dingoes. Some horses were still being used but most of the work is now done by truck or motor bikes. It was a very lonely place, schooling by radio and the flying doctor were operating. Yet this was only 300 miles from the State capital and 50 miles from a pub and a school. The situation further outback can be indescribably isolated.

2. The Ord River – Farming the Hard Way

I am a member, not paid up, of the Ord River Club situated at Kunanara in the Kimberleys, North-West Australia. It is a hot, arid and generally disagreeable place. But it became famous in the '60s at a time when panic about the future of the world's food supplies was stimulating governments and investors everywhere to start farming in areas which had previously been left severely alone. The reason for disregarding the Ord was quite simply that there are two distinct kinds of tropics. There are the lush, forested tropics you get in West Africa, Malaysia and Queensland. Parts of Queensland have constant rainfall. And there are the arid tropics with seasonal rain as in the Ord, which has a long period of summer drought which effectively destroys the chance of perpetual greenery. I'm certain that early mariners from places like Indonesia knew Australia long before the Europeans came there. Even the Dutch had found it 200 years before settlement, on their way to the East Indies, but had not landed and colonised because they just did not like what they saw of the country and its inhabitants.

The Ord had been settled in the last years of the 19th century though, having been allocated to various grazing and farming interests, of which the most notable were the Durack family. To get an idea of early pioneering in the north of Australia the account of this family's exploits in the book *Kings in Grass Castles* makes fascinating reading. After an abortive attempt to keep sheep there, the Duracks drove cattle across from Queensland, established a cattle station, which still exists, and tried to make an economy work without much success.

What beat everybody were the great distances – the Ord is 500 miles south of Darwin, 2,000 miles north of Perth and 2,000 miles across country to Queensland. This made it almost certain that only in times of the very highest prices for cattle could the high costs of transport or even walking the cattle be overcome. However, during the '50s the Australian Government, mindful of the threat of expansion from Malaysia, China and other sources of hordes of yellow people, decided that something should be done about the area. First there was a commercial American exploitation of an area near Darwin for growing rice. 'Rum Jungle' it was called and it came to naught. First of all it was hard to find a market for rice, and, more important, great flocks of geese came along and gobbled up the rice, making it impossible to secure a harvest.

At the same time a research station was set up on the Ord to see what could be grown there. Theoretically almost anything could, provided water from the Ord River could be stored and used during the dry season. So glowing were the reports from the station that funds were eventually found to build a dam across the Ord to hold back the water. The land was cleared and a number of pilot farms established. At the time of my visit there were about a dozen. But the cost of maintaining them and selling their produce was such that one Australian economist said it would be better to pay them £5,000 a year each to go and live there and do nothing. An independent view was needed. So with the blessing of the West Australian Government I flew up with Ronie to have a look on my way to Darwin and England.

We flew in a Fokker Friendship, which landed at a number of intermediate stops in the dark with no more to guide it than a couple of flares and the plane's own headlamps. This plane was called The Swan and belonged to a private airline. There was a tale that one visitor to the north, having been flown on and on by a plane called The Swan each time he moved, asked the pilot why all the company's planes had the same name. He was told there was only one. Half the cabin had seats, the other half was for storing cargo, anything from fresh vegetables to car springs – highly necessary in the pioneering north.

The airports were all the same. A small office and a sun shelter under which the passengers sat alongside a rusty iced-water dispenser which did not work. The view around was always the same too – scrub, dust and the lethargic attempts of the ground crews, always about three, to unload then reload the cargo, which all appeared to have been packed in the wrong order. I remarked how much better it would be if coloured people, used to the sun, could have done this work, instead of the polyglot European immigrants who were employed. But then I reflected that coloured people don't work very fast in the heat either, and who could blame them. We eventually reach Kunanara, and were taken to the Club and told to make ourselves at home.

The pioneers were a very mixed lot. At that time the Government reduced taxes on those prepared to live and work in the tropics. Then again, communication with the other centres of population was extremely bad. There was no telephone, only a wireless telegraph system which worked sometimes. So it became a haven for those who wanted to escape from a sour marriage, perhaps, or from the police, who only pursued really serious criminals. Or perhaps they just wanted to make some money.

In the Club bar that evening I met a gentleman who told me he was a surveyor building roads. He was up there for the specific purpose of saving enough money to develop further a shaft he had in a prospective gold mine at a place called Marble Bar in Western Australia. Marble Bar is considered the hottest place on the Australian continent. Looking at me with gleaming eyes, he extolled the benefits of the investment of even another £1,000 in his hole in the ground. 'You see, Mr Cherrington', he said, 'most people think that a gold-bearing reef runs dead straight. If it starts at an angle of 45 degrees to the surface, it will carry on that way to the centre of the earth. But this one, I am certain, is broken and is already turned on itself and pointing upwards. If only I could bore another 100 to 150 ft, I would be a rich man. I only need another £2,000 to make absolutely sure.'

He was a man in his 50's, so I asked him what his wife thought about this. To which he replied, 'But she married a gold prospector with her eyes open and everyone knows what that means.' During our stay we heard many personal stories, including one from a lady who insisted on bombarding Ronie for several years afterwards with accounts of her marital problems, from which she had escaped for a brief spell to be employed in the Club.

I thought the Ord an area of great attraction. Largely a plain surrounded by rocky outcrops several hundred feet high, in certain lights it had an extraordinary beauty and variety of colour. The potential farming area is huge. Even with the preliminary dam some 12,000 acres could have been irrigated. And there is no doubt that almost anything could be grown there. But though it was virgin soil there were problems. The main crop when I was there was cotton, and it grew well. But for some reason a grub which lives on cotton had been living on a weed in the Ord district ever since the world began. As soon as the cotton was planted, it moved over. So immediately the virgin farming enterprise

Cotton will grow on the Ord River, but this bug killed it all in the end.

Sugar cane will also grow on the Ord.

The Flinders range, South Australia.

The graveyard of a deserted township near Blinman, S.A.

needed a sophisticated crop-spraying set-up, because the cotton needed to be sprayed once a week for about 12-15 weeks.

This was a great blow to the administrators of the scheme and to the farmers. Organising the spraying programme made great demands on nervous energy, I was told, and nervous energy in an average heat of some 95 degrees F. with high humidity was in very short supply. The farmers were having a rough time, I thought, and their wives even more so. Their houses were not yet air-conditioned, and I found the heat some of the most unpleasant I have ever experienced. It is no fun changing a tractor tyre, moving irrigation pipes, cooking, or even doing the books with sweat pouring off one's nose. Some of them were suffering from prickly heat and the only relief would be a picnic on the banks of the Ord River itself or on the lake behind the dam.

The cost of getting supplies in by air was fantastic. A cabbage costing sixpence in Perth cost three shillings and sixpence on the Ord. Fertilisers and machinery were shipped more cheaply from Japan or Europe than from Perth or Darwin, owing to the very high cost of Australian shipping. The awful thing about it was that almost everything grown experimentally, or like the cotton commercially, on the Ord could be grown as well and more cheaply in the more settled areas of New South Wales and Queensland, where irrigation water is available. This is a fact common to nearly all the schemes which have been attempted over the years as a short cut to instant farming. I have mentioned the Ord in particular because I went there while it was working. But the most notable fiasco was the groundnut scheme.

This was set up by the British Government after the War with the best intentions in parts of what is now Tanzania to grow groundnuts or earth nuts. The groundnut is a valuable source of oil and protein material which the world was very short of after the last war. So, advised by a number of experts, the Government instituted the cultivation of some 100,000 acres of groundnuts. Though the failure of the scheme was probably inevitable and an indictment of a bureaucratic approach to farming, it was clear to my mind that it was also due to some very bad technical advice.

The groundnut fruits, as its name implies, beneath the surface of the soil. This means that for successful harvesting the soil should be friable. But I discovered that in many of the groundnut areas the soil was not friable, but was a cap of clay which set hard after the rains and made harvesting or even growth of the nuts extremely difficult. I said this to one of the many experts called in by the Government after the scheme had really gone wrong, and suggested that instead of groundnuts they should try vegetable oil from sunflowers, which as everybody knows like sun and don't ripen in the ground. This recommendation was made and I was interested to see in the next report that sunflowers were being tried with increasing success in place of groundnuts. However, the sunflowers were thought about too late. Wartime scarcities were filled from more traditional sources, and the groundnut scheme vanished more or less without a trace.

The Ord is doing roughly the same, as I understand it now. The bug has beaten the cotton and the latest scheme is for sugar. But for the last few years sugar has been under a growing quota and would be unlikely to be commercially viable because of distance under almost any system. But there is one other lesson which makes the Ord almost worthwhile. It showed without question that farming – highly productive farming – could be carried on in this unlikely place if ever there was a demand for it. The world need never starve, despite what Malthus said.

3. A Right and Left – Pheasant and Kangaroo!

On Boxing Day 1957 I shot a pheasant and, on New Year's Day 1958, a kangaroo. In between I had quite an interesting time. I was setting out to revisit the scenes of my emigration to the Antipodes, in the guise of a journalist and broadcaster. In other words, I hoped that the trip would pay for itself, which in the end it did. I had a commission to write articles and to do some filming, using the local broadcasting organisations' facilities for the BBC.

I always think this form of travel is the best there is. If a paper or the BBC has contributed to the enterprise it will probably make sure that whatever is sent in is published, and it gives a purpose to the whole exercise, which is lacking in ordinary tourism.

I remember when I was recovering from illness a friend came to cheer me up. For my convalescence he recommended a Mediterranean sunspot where less than 20 yds separated the beach, the bar and the bed, a prospect which immediately filled me with horror. Once, in the course of a journey through Jamaica, I had to spend a night in a beach hotel on the north coast. There I saw the package tourists wallowing in the tepid water, reading paperbacks and drinking planter's punches. This could all be done in a warm bath at home, leaving even more cash for the essential alcohol to keep the metabolism working.

I flew to Australia by QANTAS in a Constellation aircraft, which chugged along at about 10,000 ft and gave a splendid view of the country beneath us. I had been studying the world wheat situation, and when we flew over Turkey was interested to see the erosion which that country's sudden emergence as a wheat exporter had caused. Hillsides, it seemed to me, were overwhelming the villages, and it did not surprise me when Turkey left the exporters' club shortly afterwards.

We had been joined in Rome by refugees from the Russians'

Hungarian takeover, who were setting out to Australia to make new lives. They were happy to be leaving Europe but they were troubled and frightened people with practically no English, though one or two spoke a little German. These people had families, including quite small babies, and while flying between Karachi and Calcutta one of the babies turned green. There was a general alarm on the plane. Hostesses rushed about with oxygen, and almost everyone was implored to help. My only contribution was a knowledge of German from school with which I could communicate the bare essentials – and they were essentials. Anyway, the Captain radioed ahead for a doctor to meet the plane at Calcutta.

When we got there, the doctor just did not want to know. He could only certify that the baby was free of any infectious disease that could endanger the health standards of his country. The baby had meanwhile regained its normal colour, but a mass meeting of the passengers informed the Captain it would be criminally wrong if this prospective Australian citizen failed to get there. I even claimed a relationship with *The Times* and BBC which would noise abroad the iniquity of condemning this unfortunate infant to death should we take off with it. In the emotion of the moment I did not enlighten them that my connection with both these organs was agricultural. It served me right, because the Captain then decided that as I spoke some German I should go with the parents to a British doctor who was established in the Great Eastern Hotel. I agreed to go, provided he allowed the First Officer to come with me. I did not want to be left in Calcutta while he flew on. So together with a Eurasian ground hostess we set off in a sort of minibus with no glass, but just bars for windows.

The way from Dum Dum airport to the centre of Calcutta provided every feature of Indian life from corpses in the gutter upwards. The cultural shock has endured to this day. I have never seen such abject misery and squalor in quite a wide experience of life. The crowning moment came when the hostess said that the baby had just died in her arms and what should she do. By this time the parents were in a state of shock, and even my statement that we believed the baby dead produced no reaction at all. We had the bus stopped, and it was immediately surrounded by crowds of beggars of both sexes, the women thrusting their scrofulous children up to the windows.

We had a Thermos with some warm water and milk powder, so I suggested to the hostess that we mix a little in the Thermos cup and give the baby a drink. I was not quite certain that it was indeed dead, and decided to give it a go. There was little else one could have done. But, said the hostess, there is no bottle. So I dipped my unhygienic little finger in the mixture and let it dribble into its mouth. Sure enough, though only two months old, it gave a sort of gurgle and took quite a bit of interest. After this, it was soon sick, so naturally we decided it was indeed worth getting to the doctor. This gentleman saw us at once, and on learning that the baby had turned green said at once that it was a blue baby and should never fly. But why, I asked, were they called blue babies when in fact they turned green? Everyone, he told me, knew that a blue baby was in fact green. So the family, still in a state of shock, was dumped at the Great Eastern Hotel, and the aircraft took off four hours late.

Some years later on another QANTAS flight I met the First Officer again, by this time a Captain, and he reminded me of our experience. He told me he had flown the family on to Australia about a month later. So if ever the child of some Hungarian immigrants becomes either the most notorious character in the nation or saves it from unutterable chaos, I deserve the praise or the blame, because without my little finger it would never have got there in the first place! On the next leg of this interminable flight I was talking to a Singapore Chinese woman who was, she told me, going to New Zealand to marry a New Zealand Chinese, an arranged marriage if ever there was one. What, I asked her, had she been doing in England? Learning to be a midwife. I asked why she hadn't helped with the baby. 'It is not a Chinese custom', was all she said!

I was met at Sydney by an Australian representative of the BBC. It was midnight, the temperature was about 90 deg F. and I was dead tired after 60 hours' travel. 'Have you seen our Harbour, John? . . . our circular Quay, and what about Kings Cross, a sort of all-night Piccadilly?' I hadn't, but I did, finishing up with rock oysters at an all-night café on the Cross. There was something rather raffish about the Cross, the nearest thing to Buenos Aires in Australasia. But you had to eat to drink, and in those days the bars were closed at 6 pm.

This licensing law led to two methods of getting in the night's ration of alcohol. The '5 o'clock swill', where drinkers hurried from the office into a bar to ingest as much as they could before closing time, which was rigidly enforced. Australian beer is served ice cold, the temperature is high and the drink only hits you after you have had a few. Road deaths used to be at their highest around 7 pm. The other method was to book a hotel room. Then drink could be served at all hours. I encountered the second variety at the Old Australia Hotel, where I finally crawled to rest at about two in the morning. There were three of these room parties on my landing, and the singing, the quarrelling and the flushing of lavatories continued until dawn.

So it was with difficulty I caught my plane the next day for Adelaide. The flight was very rough and I began to think of metal fatigue while the aircraft flung itself around the sky. However, having flown from Europe I had my plane stomach and was eating my lunch alongside the co-pilot as we were going in to Broken Hill. As he left me to help with the landing, he advised me to watch, it should be good he said. I don't know what he meant by good. But we seemed to come out of the clouds at about 0 feet and did a turn on our wingtip, which seemed to touch the ground. As I watched this, completely petrified, I saw a rabbit, equally petrified, which seemed to be having to duck to avoid the wing. After we had landed I asked the pilot why he had risked it. 'One of our bosses was on board, and we were going to show the bastard what we could do', he said.

Bert met me at Adelaide, burnt almost black by the sun. 'You look pale, John. Are you ill, John?' 'All I need,' I said 'is a night's rest – or, better still, two'. We drove 70 miles to his home, met the family, and I fell asleep over supper. I slept badly that night. Rabbits and wing tips, to say nothing of green babies, processed through my subconscious. There was a banging on the door. 'Out you get, John, and help me inseminate some ewes'. Bert was a progressive Australian farmer and progressive people are difficult to keep up with at the best of times.

Outside the sun was fully out at 6 am and I had my first look at the Australian countryside in summer. In fact, I have never seen it at any other time. I was shocked. Even in the Argentine I had not seen anything so dry. Everything was burnt to a pale yellow colour. There was not one green thing. The eucalyptus were ragged and the leaves a tired looking brown. We climbed on to horses and rode off to muster the ewes. They were pedigree Dorset Horns and appeared to have little but dust to eat.

As we eased the mob along, one of them rolled over and died without a struggle. I got off my horse to have a look at her. She was as fat as the proverbial pig. 'What do you think she died of, Bert?' I asked. 'I suppose she could not face it any more.' I must say I did not blame her. In actual fact she probably died because she was too well fed. The dusty soil held a great stock of clover burrs or seeds from the subterranean clover and other vetches. These form the main summer feed as long as they don't sprout. Later in Australia I saw flocks of sheep and cattle grazing in a cloud of dust and looking very well on it.

On approaching a gateway, Bert asked me to ride ahead and open it. This I tried to do, but it was stiff, so, in the best cowboy fashion I swung my legs over the horse's back to jump to the ground. I never touched it. Glancing down, I saw a snake and by some feat of extraordinary agility was back in the saddle and galloping away. 'Christ!' said Bert, 'you seen a ghost?' 'No ghost,' I said, when I could get my breath back, 'there is a bloody great snake there.' 'Pick it up by the tail and crack it then', he said. 'That,' I replied, 'is something I would sooner watch than try myself.' So he rode up, inspected the snake, and then got off. But he did not make a move to catch its tail. He found a rock and staggered towards the snake with it giving the reptile time to run away. 'Cowardly bastard', said Bert. As we were riding on I asked him what would have happened if the snake had bitten one of us. 'All Australians are equipped for snake bites', he said, and produced a very rusty razor blade. 'You just slash the leg or whatever down to the bone, suck the poison out, then pray.' 'It's a bugger,' he added, 'when you get bitten in the arse and have no one with you.'

After breakfast he said, 'It's too hot to work. I promised Murray you would go and visit him.' This was where one of my sons had been working and had in fact become attached to a daughter, but they parted by mutual consent. By the time I reached Murray's it was very hot indeed – 'century temperature' they called it. Inside the house was a windowless room designed for the hot weather where Murray and I sat making conversation, drinking lemonade. It was a teetotal household. I was trying to charm Mrs Murray who obviously looked on me as the despicable block from which an unappreciative chip had come. I should say here that I sent four sons to Australia with orders to marry the only child of a rich squatter. This was the only case where my instructions were even half followed. I particularly remember the way Mrs Murray made her daughters always wear hats in the sun. Leathery complexions get you nowhere in Australian society. A middle-aged Welsh spinster had just collared their next door farmer's son.

When I got back that evening I was taken to a New Year's Eve party at a neighbour's. We got there in darkness and the house was surrounded by parked cars. Through their windows I could see large shapes in a sort of dance. They seem to start love early in the evening, I thought, but it turned out these were the children, for whom there were no sitters-in, a feature I noticed throughout Australia. The main party drink was beer and sherry, not a very good mix on a tired constitution, and as soon as 1958 was in I began to think of bed. Suddenly the temperature dropped, literally as fast as that, and Bert said, 'A southerly. We'll go bush tomorrow.'

When we got home I went to bed, but Bert and his two sons began to get the car ready. That is, they mended a puncture, and attached a water bag in front of the radiator. These water bags are an essential part of Australian motoring. Being canvas, they were supposed to cool the water, and no one was supposed to go off the main roads without one. Awful tales were told of those who had perished because they had had a puncture a few miles from help. The alternative was to drink the radiator water.

The plan was to drive north beyond Port Augusta on the road to Alice Springs, then swing east towards Broken Hill. The road to the Port was through farming country, burnt brown with tired eucalyptus and very little happening at all. New Year's Day was Bert's explanation. We soon had a puncture, and changed a completely bald tyre for an even balder one with the canvas showing. I insisted we stop and buy a new one. 'Waste of time', said Bert. So I bought it. After Port Augusta the road wound through some fairly well treed country, with obvious signs of settlement. Rusty ploughs, threshing machines and other tackle were lying around and there were remains of houses. Some of these had been recently repaired and had a familiar look. 'I have seen these before', I said. 'You would have,' said Bert. 'This is where they filmed *Robbery under Arms.*' I took a photo of the churchyard, graves circa 1850, the stones brought out from England as ballast for the wool clippers, I was told.

This area had been settled for wheat growing, but the last of the settlers had left in the thirties. A 6 in. rainfall had beaten them, and the country was reverting to salt and bluebush and would carry about one Merino wool-growing sheep to 10 acres. We saw no sheep, but we did see some kangaroos. The boys began to shoot at them and actually shot some. I was given the rifle and told to aim it at one standing and looking at me from about 25 yds. I shot it, was photographed with my foot on it, and have been ashamed of myself ever since. But it must be said that kangaroos *had* to be shot because they were starving the sheep.

As dusk was falling we reached a town – Blinman, with a store, a railway station and a hotel. The proprietor, a tall fresh-faced, Irish-looking man, was standing at the door as we drew up. 'Any rooms?' asked Bert. 'Yes', he said. 'Go to the men's room and grab any unoccupied beds.' It was just like a school dormitory with a row of beds and lockers, and an ablution block at one end. We grabbed our beds, had a wash and came downstairs. 'Right?' he asked us. 'Right', we said. 'Good! Dinner will be served between 6 and 7.30, but if you are down after 6.15 you won't get a bloody sausage.' And he continued, 'We are honest here.

Leave your shoes outside the bedroom if you like. They won't be stolen but they won't be cleaned either.'

After breakfast, steak and two eggs, we set out eastwards along little more than a trace through the scrub and bush. However, road finding isn't hard in Australia. There is no system of collecting empties after use, so beer bottles are simply thrown away. They were almost touching along this track, with great heaps at the gates where tired drivers had stopped to refresh themselves. The country here was hilly, the foothills of the Flinders Ranges, and we passed an occasional stream or creek, easily found by the line of tall trees along their banks. Some of them still held water, and we swam in one, and tried to shoot duck flighting from another.

There were kangaroos everywhere, but I shot no more. Instead I watched the pattern of the hills in the incredibly clear light, and the wild life which included emus and flocks of white and grey parrots or galahs which came shrieking around us. Our lunch consisted of corned beef straight from the tin and tea boiled in a billy over an open fire. We passed the occasional fence, but apart from one sheep station we saw no sign of human habitation. Our destination was Walkeringa, still on a map, but when we got there no more than a big pub and a post office.

It was dark by this time, and I banged on the door until at last an elederly lady opened it. Yes, we could have a meal, corned beef and pickles, she said. 'What about a beer, though?' 'Are you bona fide travellers?' she asked, and made us fill in a two-page form detailing our movements over the past day, and in particular the distance we had travelled. I put London, England, as my starting place, which seemed to reassure her. We asked about rooms. 'No chance', she said. 'I haven't taken anyone in for years. But if you go another hour along this track they will put you up. But mind you get there between 8 and 9. The landlord is in strife with his wife, and at 6 he goes up the road to see the engine driver's wife. His wife will let the rooms to spite him.'

Sure enough, when we got there we were let our rooms and I went to the men's ablutions for a shower. A peculiarity of Australian country hotels in those days, and perhaps even now, was that no bathroom or lavatory doors had locks on. While I was showering a very unsteady man walked in. 'I want a bath', he said. 'Wait a minute.' He advanced on me. 'Why don't you try the women's bath?' 'Is that all right?' 'I am sure it will be.' It wasn't. Screams and high-pitched abuse came from down the corridor.I slipped off to my bedroom and put the chair against the door. 'What have you been doing now?' asked Bert, who had heard the noise. 'You bloody Poms can't leave them alone, can you?'

Salt creek on the way to Esperance, Western Australia.

4. New Zealand Revisited

New Zealand today is one of the most pleasant places to live in. The scenery and the climate are marvellous, opportunities for every kind of sport are within everyone's reach, physically and financially. There is practically no unemployment and there are no great divisions of wealth and certainly little of the class structure which is Britain's greatest deficiency today. It is a country roughly the size of the British Isles but with only 3 million people. Of these some 100,000 are engaged in farming and the remainder live on their backs. Up till now they have lived very well indeed. It is a Welfare State with everyone cared for from the cradle to the grave. A socialist paradise financed by the most individualistic and conservative body of farmers it has been my fortune to meet and, at one time, to live among.

I was once a New Zealander myself. I emigrated there after leaving school, signed on for their compulsory military service, and was prepared to make my life among them. In retrospect, more than at the time, I enjoyed my two years' stay. It was of enormous benefit to me because through associating with their egalitarian attitudes I finally threw off my own inherent class prejudices. The reasons for my leaving were simple. Times were hard and there were 30,000 unemployed out of a population of one million. I could get about eight months' casual work a year on which, helped by staying with relations, I could live. Although at that time there was no formal social security as there is now, no one would be allowed to starve, or die for lack of medical help.

I was not satisfied to sit around doing very little and I could not see much prospect of getting a farm of my own which was the object of my emigrating in the first place. There was also little chance of getting into anything else. I was not conscious of the boredom or dullness of New Zealand life which many New Zealanders give as their reasons for leaving their country. For emigration is, I believe, one of the main props of New Zealand's present almost euphoric state. There are I understand never less than 50,000 young people working abroad in places as far afield as the North Sea oil rigs, Australian mines, London hospitals and British shearing gangs. Besides this temporary emigration, over 20,000 a year settle permanently in Australia.

What this means is that a very large proportion of the age group which in other countries would be questioning all aspects of society are happily occupied abroad. Were it not for this there could be just as many urban problems as there are in Britain and elsewhere. For New Zealand is now an urban society. Most of the industry has centred in Auckland Province where a third of the 3 million population live. Wellington, the capital, is the seat of the bureaucracy and the rest are mainly centres for servicing the farming industry which by its exports is the basis of the economy.

But farming is running faster all the time to produce enough to support the rest of the population in its comfortable way of life. The problem is that 3 million New Zealanders have a standard of life equivalent to the best, but the ingredients – cars, television and almost everything else – have to be imported. This is paid for by the energies of fewer than 100,000 on the land and in the ancillary industries. If the country had been simply one very large farm, it is probable that the total population needed to service the farming industry could be fewer than a million or so. The problem is compounded by the fact that New Zealand is a very long way from the markets which were originally developed in Britain, Europe and the United States. This factor, which the Australian historian Geoffrey Blamey called 'the tyranny of distance', means that exports which carry heavy transport costs should be of low volume and high value.

Blamey was writing about Australia and instanced gold and wool as viable export products for that country. New Zealand has wool, still a fairly high value low volume product. But meat is nothing like as valuable intrinsically and costs a great deal in proportion to export. For instance, in 1981 a New Zealand farmer was getting about £7 for each of his lambs sent to slaughter. This cost £4 to slaughter and put aboard ship and no less than another £7 to reach the wholesale stage in the overseas market. New Zealand slaughter costs are the highest in the world but most of the money remains in the New Zealand economy. The rest goes to shippers and traders based abroad.

But these export earnings are not enough to support the present style of living. Since 1979 the balance of payments has been getting worse, though this has been glossed over by allowing a gentle devaluation of the currency month by month. The result is that imports of essentials like farm machinery and fertilisers and the cars and such like which are the fundamentals of the good life, cost more New Zealand dollars each month. They still come in, though in smaller quantities, but the increases in prices spark off wage claims. One of the reasons for the high cost of slaughtering is that the slaughtermen strike regularly for higher pay just at the beginning of the killing season.

Farmers can't ask for higher prices in these circumstances. Their reaction is to produce more and more each year. The whole farming economy is devoted to lowering costs by increasing production. For instance, if lambs are a bad trade, just increase the size of the flock and have more lambs to sell another year. Most New Zealand farm advisory work centres on increasing production and productivity on the country's grassland, which is some of the best in the world. This suits the farmer's temperament. He is proud of his independence and most scornful when he talks of what he believes to be the subsidised farming of the Common Market. He thinks he has been placed by the Almighty in a situation where he is the most economic producer in the world and that should be enough to ensure him, and New Zealand, a place in the sun.

However independence is not enough. For several years farm output was suffering because of the impossibility of financing increasing output, so the government of the day in 1975 instituted a system of guaranteed prices. This was bitterly attacked, particularly by the sheep and cattle farmers. Part of the trouble was that the government was Labour, but the system has been carried on and even reinforced by the present National or Conservative government. I was in New Zealand at the time of the first measures and it seemed that the farmers' opposition was not as wholehearted as its leaders would have one believe. The dairy farmers were for it and so were many of the younger farmers, because they were suffering the economic pressures much more than the well established ones.

There always had been a marked social division between the sheep and cattle graziers and the dairy farmers. I lived and worked among the former and it was clearly understood that dairy farmers were a much lower class. Their children were said never to be so bright at school and they exploited their wives unmercifully just for the sake of the monthly cheque. The same division used to exist between arable farmers and cow keepers in Wiltshire when I started farming. Dairy farmers were always under the pressure of the twice daily milking chore, and also because of many years of chronically low prices. So they formed co-operatives which grew into the New Zealand Dairy Board which, under farmer control, markets produce from the farm to the consumer and does a first-rate job. The graziers on the other hand saw no need to co-operate with each other or anyone else. A proposal to unify wool marketing so that it was all sold through one single channel was defeated after the most bitter debate. Their meat marketing is a shambles. Not in terms of quality, of course – these standards are rigidly enforced – but by exploitation by almost anyone else.

You must understand that the average New Zealand farmer has traditionally not been encouraged to do his business as we do in Britain. There are few markets; much of his finance comes, not from banks, but from what are called pastoral companies, which finance the stock and other resources needed. The companies do much of the marketing and supplying. I am not suggesting that they were exploiting farmers in any dishonest sense but they certainly stopped him from doing his own thing. Many of these companies used to be British owned, as were the main meat exporters which had direct links with the British market. Even the pricing of New Zealand lamb in Britain is at the mercy of the exporters, who control many of the British outlets.

I started reporting on the New Zealand scene many years ago and seized on this aspect as one of the major weaknesses of the country's and the farmer's economy. I soon found that critics, even those as well disposed as I was, and still am, are not appreciated. My articles were reprinted in the New Zealand papers and violently attacked, I imagine by interests keen to maintain the status quo. The crux of this particular controversy came when I suggested that if the present attitude to marketing was allowed to persist New Zealand might find herself a sort of Falkland Islands of the South Pacific with no alternative but to become the seventh state of the Australian Commonwealth. This led to questions in Parliament, and a general condemnation by the New Zealand establishment, for questioning the rightness of everything being done.

Of course, they were well within their rights to attack my presumption. But the fact is that there is no debate in New Zealand society as we know it in this country. Even Parliament is remarkably well mannered. The recent agitation about the Springboks' tour is the first time in my memory that an issue has led to mass demonstrations and fighting with police on what might be called a moral issue. It could also signal a split between the rural population, fanatical rugby supporters, and city dwellers who are developing an awareness of what is going on in the world outside and are prepared to stand up for their principles. Not that they did not have

Farm walk in hill country, New Zealand.

Horse shoeing on a sheep farm, New Zealand.

The author and his son Tom panning gold in Skipper's Creek, N.Z. No luck!

Dairying in the North Island.

principles in the past. They have been keen supporters of Britain as long as I can remember.

In the last two world wars New Zealand was more committed to our support than any other country of the Commonwealth. In the post-war years they deliberately took lower prices than they need have done just to show this support. For this reason Britain's joining the Common Market and subsequently reducing New Zealand exports has severely shaken their trust. They have not been so violently critical of the EEC and all its works as have the Australians. They still feel that as long as they don't make too much fuss all will be well. For many years I have put New Zealand's case in the Press and elsewhere and have always suggested that they should press the matter more vehemently before they lose it all. The reply was an unequivocal admonition not to make too much fuss, that they were being looked after and had nothing to fear. In terms of market share they have been forced to accept a position which could go very much against them.

But why do I bother? There are many other lively and more interesting countries to visit and write about. Places where epoch-making changes are taking place. There are no problems of starvation, of unemployment and of great social injustice in New Zealand. Yet I have been there every five or six years for the last 30 years and hope to go again and again. Contrary to many people, I don't find the country or the people dull to be among. I am sure this adjective is a reflection of the critic's own character. After all, there are plenty of towns and areas of Britain which are very dull to live in, even provincial, lacking the sophistication of London. Yet in every population grouping there are a whole host of different interests. It is possible to lead an interesting life in almost any society. It is simply a matter of seeking out like-minded people and fostering these interests.

Many deplore the lack of what they call culture, with the big 'C'. I would be the first to admit that there is nothing like the London or New York stage in New Zealand and that television and radio are as banal as they are at home. But how many people in Britain really enjoy these things and seek them out? For that matter, why does the Arts Council have to subsidise the theatre, music and the ballet? If the British were as desperate about culture as all that, these enterprises would be highly profitable. But there is no shortage of books and the newspapers are good and carry a great deal of foreign news. There is plenty of life for those who wish to find it.

Of course, for those who can't help themselves things can be pretty dreary. A wet Sunday afternoon in Invercargill or Wanganui would drive anyone to suicide. But then so would Reading or Halifax have done before Sunday trading restrictions were lifted in Britain. My advice to travellers to those towns is to make their own amusements. Even 30 years ago bars closed promptly at 6 p.m. and the last order for dinner had to be given by 6.30 in quite big hotels. After that the dining-room doors were firmly shut. I once travelled the length of the North Island with two distinguished scientists. We missed every meal deadline in three whole days and had to live on coffee and biscuits and snacks at cafés which were quite frightful in those days. Now things have very much changed. Meals can be had in most places, ungrudgingly served, and New Zealand wines are very good and very cheap. But there are undoubted stresses developing.

For many years New Zealand's relations with the Maoris were an example to the world. They have full equality with the whites and many take the fullest advantage of it. But there is no doubt that economically they are the underdogs and resent it. In 1981 the celebrations of the Treaty of Waitangi, where the Maoris made peace with the whites, were disrupted by vehement protests. Maoris are becoming aware that they gave away a lot at Waitangi. There are some ugly racial problems in Auckland, where there is a large Polynesian element who have the right of entry to New Zealand. These, added to Maori discontent, cannot be ignored much longer.

Then there is a danger that the continuing world recession could make it more difficult for the safety valve of emigration, permanent or temporary, to relieve the pressures that the retention in the country of all these young people would be sure to bring. But even if the social problems can be mastered, what of the economy? This seems to me to be the big question mark. Quite obviously the continuing balance of payments deficit cannot go on for ever. Much of this is made up by payments by New Zealanders for foreign travel and luxury imports, both of which make for the better life they enjoy. When I was there in early 1981 the whole atmosphere was one of a sort of Shangri-la, drifting pleasantly along without thought of tomorrow, which could be a day of reckoning. In fact at that time it was the only society in the world which seemed unaware that the recession was raging across the seas. Perhaps the 'tyranny of distance' isolates New Zealand from the world's problems as well as its markets. If this is true and permanent it is indeed a fortunate country.

PART 2: NORTH AMERICA

5. Oil-Rich Farming in Texas

I arrived in San Antonio, Texas, late in the afternoon, knowing no one and with nothing to do until the next morning, when I was due to catch a bus to the Mexican border. The hotel room was as hygienic and as empty of life as all the best American hotels are. The town itself looked far from interesting, and I was tired and fed up with being a package on a conveyor belt of American entertainment of foreign students. True, I was in my fiftieth year, rather old for a student, but not apparently too old for the English Speaking Union, who chose me, and the Ford Foundation who paid for the trip. Those chosen were not confined to farmers. All sections were represented as 'opinion-forming characters'. We were given sustenance and travel for eight weeks in the States, and a tour was laid on with the utmost of American efficiency by an organisation known as the Governmental Affairs Agency, based in Washington.

Within three days of my arrival there I had been consigned sight unseen to contacts on every step of the way, but I came to the regrettable conclusion that many of the people who looked after me were getting a per capita payment for the job. To many of them, particularly at the colleges and universities, I was just another body, 'white English speaking' for a change. But I was just such another and they showed it.

From this stricture I must exempt the English Speaking Union, who, when they could get hold of me, proved to be the most helpful people I have ever had the good fortune to encounter, and to which I have been happy to pay a subscription since. I must emphasise the effort made to contact them. For some reason the Government Affairs Institution of those days was very anti the ESU. I thought they could have done the whole thing standing on their heads. Instead, I was steadily warned against them.

Anyway, here was I resting on my solitary couch in San Antonio, or San Anton as the locals call it, when the phone rang. 'Is that you John?' 'Yes.' 'This is Richard. Be downstairs in ten minutes, we are going to a party.' Exactly ten minutes later, Richard, a dapper man in his sixties speaking with what I can only describe as a refined Texan accent, spotted me, and shook me warmly by the hand. 'Great to see you. Where in England are you from?' 'Hampshire.' 'Now isn't that great! I spent the war in Tidworth.' In his car he reminisced about Andover and Salisbury, the green fields and the trees, none of which are prominent in Texas.

'This is the club', he said, as we drew up to the sidewalk. We went inside where it was very like a St. James's Street club, except that the negro servants wore a sort of Grenadier Guards uniform. There we proceeded to meet his friends. Richard, I forgot to say, was dressed in a red tunic, and others in the party had a distinct military look. The ladies, though, were in full regalia. Drinks of surprising strength were handed round. One of the ladies attached herself to me. 'Ah, you are English. Let me hear your brogue.' Somehow the term, which I had heard before, jarred. We speak of an Irishman's brogue. But to hear my own BBC English referred to in this way made me feel as if I was an intruder from the fringes of culture. So to please her I asked the purpose of the party.

'Right now', she said, 'we are getting into the right frame of mind for the boats.' 'For the boats?' I queried. Texas is not very flush with water at the best of times. 'Yes,' she said, 'we are going on to the river to celebrate the battle of San Jacinto. The battle when the Alamo was avenged, and Texas became American.' After a while Richard grabbed me from her conversation and packed me into a car with several others. All the men, it appeared, had been in England in the war and most of them in the South as well. They had obviously enjoyed themselves – in retrospect anyway. 'Great to have you with us, John', they said.

We eventually arrived at a landing stage and boarded one of many flat bottomed boats on which was a steersman and a cook. There were benches and tables and lots and lots of drink. While waiting to cast off, my neighbour, who told me he was a banker, asked me at what age I allowed my daughter to be taken out by a young man. It's not a question of allowing, I replied, but by the time she went to university it was about right, I thought. At about 18. 'What would you do, John, if a young man brought your daughter a corsage on her twelfth birthday and took her out for the evening?' I had no idea, until I asked Richard later what a corsage was. 'A bunch of orchids', he told me. I think I told the banker tactfully that American girls matured faster than they did in Europe. Wasn't the legal age for marriage in Texas 12? 'No more', he said. 'It is 14. In the early days it was quite sensible to have the lower age as there were few white women and if they could not get a white one the locals would marry Indians or Mexicans. We could not have that'.

'Well', I said, 'in matters of children's upbringing I always leave all moral and other questions to my wife. After all, if the creator had intended man to bear and rear children he would have made some provision for it.' 'That, John, is no answer to my problems', he said. Moments later he introduced me to his wife and moved away. 'He has been talking to you about our Joanie?' 'He has,' I replied. 'And what did you tell him?' I told her. 'That was real good advice, John.' And she rubbed herself hard against me and gave me a most embarrassing kiss. Wedged against the rail I could not escape. Richard came on the scene with yet another drink. 'At home, John? That is what we Texans like to see in the guests who visit with us.'

By this time we were moving up the river, a narrow ditch between high walls. There was plenty of floodlighting and the banks and bridges were lined with great masses of people, mainly Mexican or Indian by the look of their faces. Bands were playing on some of the boats, and we were served a Mexican dish. It was very peppery, but there was plenty to drink. Wishing to maintain the bearing of a sober representative of Britain, I poured several of mine over the side. Richard did not. He shouted and danced in time to the music and conducted a band three boats away. On the tables were big dishes of frijoles, a sort of pancake used for mopping up the gravy. 'Let us feed the poor,' he shouted, and began to throw them up to the crowds on the side. They skimmed through the air quite well. Perhaps they had been specially made for this. Those on shore pelted us back.

It all went on a very long time. There seemed an inexhaustible supply of frijoles and drink. We eventually got ashore and Richard became very friendly. 'You must stay longer, John', he kept saying. 'I will call you tomorrow. We will arrange something together. I have ranches and oil wells.' The next morning I was packing to leave when the phone rang. 'John,' he said, 'I feel terrible. I don't think I can get out today at all.' 'Thank you, I enjoyed myself', I said. Before I caught the bus I went to look at the Alamo mission where some hundred Americans were massacred by Mexicans. It was a moving experience, though most of them were adventurers engaged in an enterprise of doubtful legality. How many Mexicans died at San Jacinto?

The bus set me down in the town of Del Rio after a five-hour journey through a dull plain covered for the most part in short scrub. The Rio referred to is the Rio Grande, the boundary between Texas and Mexico. The hotel was next to the bus station, and I had no sooner settled than I was routed out again by the most engaging character I had met for years. A huge man with a great smiling face, a stetson, and jeans which clung to him like skin. He introduced himself as Dink Wardlaw, farmer, rancher, wool merchant and banker in the town. 'You need refreshment', he said, as he pushed me into a chair in his living room. He put a glass full of ice and Bourbon into my hand, then pressed a switch. Immediately a foot rest extended from the chair and the whole apparatus began to shake.

I could hardly hear what he said above the rattle of my ice cubes, except that I was welcome. We would be going into Mexico for dinner that night. The next day we would be at his wool sale and see his farms, or some of them. In the car he told me more. His family had settled there after the civil war, benefiting doubtless from the battle of San Jacinto. He didn't count acreage, but he had 20,000 Angora goats for mohair – they lived well on the bushes – several thousand cattle, and some Rambouillet sheep. He was drawing royalties from several hundred small oil wells, and he expected more.

As we moved more among the ranching folk it became clear that all the cowboy pictures were real. Everyone wore a stetson and tight jeans. The only difference was that none carried guns. Except in the evenings the ladies dressed the same. In my sports coat and slacks I felt very much an outsider. But they were all very friendly, including Dink's father-in-law. A typical picture Texan, thin and gaunt with a decided eye for the girls. For these we crossed over the river into Mexico. To me it was like going back 30 years. It was just like Argentina again – poverty, earth roads, adobe houses away from the main streets, and a great succession of houses of pleasure. Here we saw a few guns. The car park attendant had a pistol and so had the police and soldiers. We had a meal and watched the dancing. The girls clung to pa-in-law like leeches and he clung to them. We were quite a large party, mostly wool buyers whom Dink had brought over to freshen up for the sale the next day. Mexican dance halls have little glamour, nor had those in Argentina. But they pleased the wool buyers, mostly from the North-Eastern States, where such goings on were not so publicly tolerated. Much of the USA displays a stern front of conventional morality, so I suppose many of these frontier Mexican towns provide a relief that they cannot get at home. Sexual satisfaction must be a major export in the north of Mexico.

At the wool sale I met a number of ranchers. They seemed to be men of

Dink Wardlaw (left) and Mexican farm hand, Texas.

Desert garden in Arizona.

Mexican shearer: he weighed over 300 lbs.

The author with a Georgian rancher.

incredible wealth, although most modest in their dress and behaviour. They were, of course, well sustained, as Dink was, by the royalties or deposits they were getting on their oil prospects. Few seemed to live on their farms. Most were in a sort of irrigated suburbia with trees and lawns in the better part of Del Rio, an oasis in the desert. I visited a couple of ranch homes in the city, one for a house-warming where the floor of the bedroom was covered with a carpet at least 4 in. thick. No bed would be necessary. Some were irrigating from artesian wells, sowing sorghum and maize and there was some dry land wheat growing. But not actually at the moment. The government was operating a 'set aside' programme, so they were being paid not to grow wheat. Yields of dry land wheat are, of course, very low and one man confessed to me his wheat paid far better under 'set aside' than it ever had when he farmed it. At the wool sale every lot was subject to sealed bids, so that no one would know what the other man was doing. There was no excitement as in a proper auction either. At the end of the day the successful bids were announced and there was a lot of leg pulling.

I liked Dink very much and when I was travelling through the States a couple of years later wrote to him and suggested I called. His widow replied. He had had a massive coronary while driving 200 miles to an uncle's funeral and by the time he had been brought to hospital it was too late.

Sometime later I was staying on a farm near Smith Centre, Kansas, which, until Hawaii became a state in its own right, was at the very centre of the United States. The farm was of about 3,000 acres. My host, Gerald's grandfather, had homesteaded 160 acres, his father had built it up to 1,000 acres, now he and his brother had the present acreage. Each morning I heard Gerald get up just after 4.30 and go out and do the chores. He and his brother milked 20 cows, fed and looked after several hundred pigs, saw that the cattle in the feed lot, about 300, had feed and hay supplies, and fed a thousand hens. Then they came into breakfast, ready to begin the day's work on the farm. They grew 600 acres of wheat but few other crops though they made a lot of lucerne hay. The wheat was grown in alternate narrow strips, a measure to combat the drought. In some cases, as in Canada, they only grew a crop every other year. This enlargement of the farm had been at the expense of many others which had been abandoned or sold in the Depression and afterwards. On every side there were empty houses, schools and churches for which there was no more need.

I went to see the grandmother, still alert and very active. Married at 14, she was 96 and remembered, she told me, the last herd of buffaloes that came through the farm. There was a lot of shouting and shooting and her husband had been fearful for his crops. This area had suffered very badly as part of the dustbowl during the Depression and only the hardiest could possibly have survived. Those that had were exceptional people, I thought, with perhaps an over-simplistic view of right and wrong. They were good because they knew they were good and that hard work and a strong faith were all that was needed for success in life. I met this attitude in other parts of the Middle West and though they appear dull and very narrow to the sophisticated, they are undoubtedly part of the backbone of America.

The Californians were very different. I visited an enterprise called the Kern County Land Co, a spread originally British in the San Joachim valley near Bakersfield. This is one of the largest farming companies in the States and was run like a modern factory. The analogy is not so far fetched as it sounds. The climate is almost predictable, a long hot period without rain for most of the year. The land was mainly share cropped, the irrigation came from wells or from the Colorado river.

When I was called at six in the morning the sky was overcast and I asked my guide if he thought it would rain. 'No,' he said emphatically, 'it never rains here in April.' Nevertheless, I said if I saw a sky like this at home I would immediately think that it was going to rain by four in the afternoon. Sure enough by four o'clock the heavens opened and it caught them all on the hop. The hay they were making for the dairies on the coast was all spoiled, the potato and onion harvests had to come to a halt, the machinery got bogged down and they were in a proper mess for the next few days.

The people I met all seemed to be employees of big businesses, either share croppers or migrant workers. They looked on the land like so much blotting paper on which they could grow heavier and heavier crops with the proper use of fertilisers, chemicals and above all water. In Georgia some weeks before I had been to a Department of Agriculture office where they were paying people *not* to grow cotton under a 'set aside' programme. In California I visited the cotton research institute where they showed farmers how to grow *more* cotton on a given acreage. Both projects were funded by the same Government agency. The Kern County Land Co certainly paid, but whether it was the farming or the fact that they had 1,700 producing oil wells I never found out. In every field you could see a pump head nodding.

The Californians seemed much less sure of themselves. I met one on the flight there who told me he was a member of something called Christian Businessmen's Fellowship. He had visited England and been shocked by the attitude of the poeple he tried to do business with. 'Tell me,' he said, 'Do British businessmen say a prayer before they start work?' I said I doubted it. 'Oh!' he told me, he and his associates always did. The chances of successful business could not be left to individuals alone. I could not see many Mid-Westerners needing divine assistance before they opened their offices. But my Californian acquaintance was certainly genuine in his beliefs. He gave me his card and invited me to stay.

Later in San Francisco I was invited to a weekend on a ranch. 'Be at this address at three o'clock with your bag.' I arrived at a rather nice town house where a cocktail party was going on. I had been having a pretty abstemious time since I left Texas and having found out that this was indeed the place I allowed myself to be entertained. After an hour or so everyone left me. Just as I was wondering if it was time to go back to the hotel and the whole thing was something of a flop or leg-pull, they all came back having changed into jeans and stetsons. We set off in a convoy of cars, over the famous harbour bridge and drove due north for 150 miles.

We eventually arrived at the ranch about dusk, when I witnessed an extremely embarrassing confrontation between the old matriarch of the place and her daughter-in-law. The latter was complaining that in allocating the bedrooms Ma-in-law was quite literally coming between her and her husband. 'How do you expect our marriage to hold together, when you won't let us sleep together', she cried. 'What would you do, Mr Cherrington?' Well, I ask you!

That night we had supper on a table which carried the largest dumb waiter I have ever seen. There were about a dozen of us there and the haunch of venison could be carved from everyone's chair. Conversation was muted and everyone had a good go at the Bourbon. Next day we played at ranching. There were a dozen calves which had been wintered in and had to be branded, earmarked and castrated having first been lassoed. Being the only professional there – even the ranch hand was very new and fainted at the sight of blood – I performed the necessary operations. This took all day and the next evening was as dreary as the previous one.

The following day we went to look at the family redwoods, a grove of marvellous trees surrounding a hunter's hut. This had a trap-door in the floor and down there was another cache of Bourbon. We drank heavily. At lunch a visitor, a doctor, asked me why the British were playing footsie with the Russians and why was the National Health Service allowing the British to die. I told him the story of a woman I had met in a train going to San Francisco whose doctor had refused to operate on her daughter for appendicitis until she had mortgaged her home to him. In the subsequent court case which she was subject to, having refused to stick to the agreement, a judge ordered her to pay it off at one dollar a month. This much upset the doctor, who stated that those who could not pay the bills really had no business living. 'That is what is wrong with you British', he declared.

But not even the rich can buy the best of service. A year or so later the matriarch invited me to stay, but when I got to San Francisco there was a message at the airport to say that she was in hospital. But her house, car and Chinese cook were at our disposal. We went to see her in hospital and found her very ill with pneumonia. This had not been diagnosed in time, because the team of her medical practice were on holiday, and there was no diagnostician at work. The Chinese cook had saved her life by carting her off to hospital and getting the resident doctors to care for her.

This cook, Ching, used to dress and talk like a stage Chinese, and entertained us by bringing everything in singly. For instance, if it was tea he would bring first a cup and then a saucer, and then another cup and so on. In the evenings, though, he would put on Western clothes and another Chinese would pick him up and drive him to the city. He had been born in San Francisco, he said, but had been to mainland China once. The trouble with the old lady, he told us, was that she was too rich – $30 million.

From San Francisco I travelled through the Rocky Mountains to Salt Lake City, home of the Mormons. My hosts, or rather hostesses, two elderly ladies, were not Mormons, and had the greatest contempt for them. When studying Mormon life, they told me, I should count the doors in their houses. If there were two doors, the man had one wife, but if there were any more, each rated an extra wife. I didn't push these researches but enjoyed the Mormon Choir and being taken around by a young non-Mormon. He told me that his grandmother had been sent out to marry a Mormon, but as the wagon train had been seized by the army she had married a soldier instead.

Religion apart, the Mormon march to Utah must have been a fantastic performance across 2,000 miles of hostile Prairie. Their settlement of the desert country could only have been achieved by a highly disciplined and devoted people. They still are, and the town is a model of cleanliness and good living though pretty dull as well. Some of the streets are the widest I have ever seen, said to be because Brigham Young liked to walk them with his dozen or so wives arm in arm. Polygamy, if it still exists, is now illegal. The only excuse I was given for it was that it was designed by God to give husbands to the widows of the Civil War. Whatever the morality, the movement was certainly a notable achievement in pioneering the West.

The Americans like their public servants to be just that. In Iowa, part of the famous corn belt, I went to a local meeting of the Kiwanis, a sort of Rotary, in the capital, Des Moines. The main speaker was the local superintendent of schools and he was telling us about a recent trip to Britain where he said children could be asked to leave their school if they failed to keep up in the examination rat race. Such a thing would never happen in Des Moines. I am sure that we should get on a lot better in Britain if we followed the same principle.

I stayed several times at colleges or universities. Most of them were what they call land grant colleges, to which everyone has a right to go, but most drop out after a couple of years. A feature of them was the number of young married women, pregnant and with families on the campus. The refectories were staffed by them and I asked one what she was studying. 'Just putting my man through school', she told me. There is a lot of difference between these state colleges and what are called the Ivy League establishments, such as Yale and Harvard, and it is a difference which is not confined to the academics. I once tried to cash a cheque in a bank in Massachusetts, and although it was an official cheque forming part of my grant, the Yankee teller would have nothing of it. In the end he asked me where I was staying. I told him Amherst. 'Good', he said, and then 'You don't mean the State College?' 'I do', I replied. There are two Amhersts and I was staying in the wrong one.

I spoke to several classes, which used to be summoned by bells, just like school. There were two features which I found rather off-putting. Some of the students had transistors with earplugs and were beating time to the music, and couples were going in for heavy petting – the technical term – on the back seats. I gained the attention of the lovers by telling them of a South Sea tribe I had visited who were compelled to make love in public as a cure for possible impotence, but could make no headway with the radio buffs.

6. Canada – North of the Border

In the autumn of 1970 I was reading in the *Wall Street Journal* that Canadian farmers were having such a hard time selling their wheat that they were paying their children's college fees and other things with bushels of wheat, not dollars. This looked interesting, so without more ado I managed to get the editor of *The Financial Times* to send me there to report on the situation. It appeared to be very like that operating in the depression of the 'thirties, when a good deal of this sort of barter went on.

At the time I knew very little about Canada. Some distant relatives had emigrated there at the turn of the century, and the reports that filtered back spoke of icy winters and hardships which made the experiences of the Great War, to which some of them returned, look like easy street in comparison. I knew that the Prairies were frozen for much of the winter, and that the growing season was no more than three months. But the wheats produced were of the very highest quality, though they often had to wait under snow until the spring to be thrashed out.

Ronie, my wife, and I landed in Winnipeg on 13 October. The temperature was below freezing and it was snowing quite strongly. In fact, it was snowing or freezing most of the fortnight we were there. Winnipeg is the capital of Manitoba, which gives its name to some of the best Canadian wheats. However, comparatively little wheat is grown there, but it remains the headquarters of the Canadian Wheat Commission. This organisation controls the marketing of all Canadian wheat, and obviously had to be my first port of call, although it would have been better had I travelled through the growing areas first.

I had briefed myself fairly well before leaving, and had arranged to interview the Chief Commissioner, Mr Bill Macnamara, the morning after my arrival. I was also working for the BBC and collected a Canadian crew from the broadcasting studios there. There is something about agricultural cooperatives which gives their executives delusions of grandeur. Wherever I have been, the headquarters of cooperatives worldwide seem to have been designed with status in mind. The Canadian Wheat Board was no exception. The main offices were on the top floor and furnished in what could only be described as a monumental style, with solid timber chairs which could bear the weight of the big men of the Prairies. Bill Macnamara was in every sense a big man, exuding an air of confidence, even complacency.

After discussing the world wheat market, which in his view was being ruined by price-cutting by wealthier countries like the United States – the EEC was not doing too much of it at that time – I came to the nub of my visit. Canadian farmers did not seem to be very happy, according to the newspapers I had purchased that day. Was it true that they were only being allowed to sell six bushels an acre of their crop, and many had several years' wheat in store and not paid for? Was it true that in order to raise some cash, they had created a black market in grain, selling it for a dollar a bushel to 'feed lot' operators and poultry farmers, against all the rules?

There were murmurs, he conceded, but they did not amount to anything. 'Have you, my boy,' (I was at least 60 by then but I still felt like a boy in front of his massive confidence). 'Have you ever read the good book, the Bible?' I conceded that I had. 'Well,' he said, 'you remember the story of the seven fat years and the seven lean years?' 'Yes', I replied. 'Well,' he said, 'you know Canadian farmers have had their fat years in the past, and they have had their lean years. They are going through the lean years now, but the good times will come back, and they will be all the better for not having got too soft.'

Just fancy a British or any other farmer's leader speaking like this in public. The interview was to be shown in part on Canadian TV. The explanation was that although Bill had been chosen by the Government for his job as Commissioner, the wheat farmers paid his salary. In fact, the more I looked into it, the happier I felt that I was farming in Britain and not Canada. There was at that time no Government help for farmers, though it was altered soon afterwards. They were on their own.

They had to sell their wheat through the Wheat Commission and their deliveries were controlled by the Board, which allocated space at the silos, or elevators as they are called, which are such a feature of the countryside. The farmer was paid a sum on delivery, and the rest arrived in dribs and drabs over the next three years or so. The Australians deal with wheat in the same way.

Very few farmers stored their wheat under cover. Some just left heaps in the fields where the combines were emptied, others made great stacks in their farmyards. On one farm I visited, the farmer let his dog off for a run, and it galloped up over the heap which must have been at least 15 ft high and 30 yd long. 'Damn the brute', said the farmer. 'He will break the crust'. This he showed me was a layer of wheat about 2 in thick which formed over the surface of the heap. Being slightly damp it was able to shed the water when it rained. It rained very seldom, he told me. Usually the moisture fell as snow which blew off in the winter gales. This particular heap had been in his yard for three years and under the crust was as sweet as the day it had been cut.

Before going on to Saskatchewan, the centre of wheat growing, we filmed a farmer in the Red River Valley, south of Winnipeg. The soil here is a very fine black soot – quite the best way to describe it. The farmer we visited had 3,000 acres, all arable, which he worked with his son and one man. He was harvesting potatoes the day we saw him, but had had to wait until the frost had gone out of the ground before he could get his harvester to work. When he got going, it was at about 8 mph, harvesting straight into a lorry which was going to take the spuds to a processing co-op which he and three other farmers had built. There they would be turned into mash to be sent to Britain.

His other crops were wheat, sunflower and rape seed, together with some barley. The interesting thing about this was that though there was quite a sprinkling of snow, he wasn't a bit worried that some of his wheat and all his sunflowers were unharvested. It was the most beautiful land to work, and had the climate been even temperate would have been a joy to farm.

The hotel where we stayed in Regina, Saskatchewan, had a turret and from its top storey I looked both east and west along the main road which disappeared into infinity in each direction. I had always imagined the Prairies were flat like the Argentine plain, but they are gently rolling and quite broken by swamps and gulleys. It was only from ground level that I got the impression of a flat land.

Saskatchewan is basically wheat country. The farms were talked of in 'sections', each of a square mile (640 acres). The original division of the land was a quarter section per original farmer, which they were able to acquire with very little capital but a lot of hard work. The land was originally settled along the railways. Each railway company had the right to allocate land and the silos were spaced along the tracks. If the land was good there were a lot of them, if it was poor, they were fairly well scattered.

No farmer could draw any money for his grain unless it had been deposited in the silo. When I was there the deliveries were limited to six bushels an acre, simply because the sales slump of that time precluded the emptying of the silos. So the blockage ran back to the farms, like putting a plug in a bath and seeing the water back up.

I called at an elevator, as the silos are called, and in the agent's office met a number of farmers. They were sitting round the stove drinking coffee and smoking, and did not seem to be complaining too much. One man said he would not plant any crop at all the next year. He would live on his savings and spend the time mulching his land. In this area moisture is very slight and usually comes in winter as snow. The practice is to crop every other year anyway, and the whole purpose of cultivation is to conserve moisture.

The wheat is harvested to leave a very long stubble in which what weeds there were are allowed to grow. The stubble is left standing through the winter to catch the snow, instead of allowing it to be blown off. The following spring the land is cultivated to get the trash into the top soil, and if there is more weed growth it is again mulched down into the soil. It was then sown the following spring. Sowing was often very late, and I was told that a June frost was not uncommon, and could ruin the crop or reduce yields to nothing.

Yields were very low by our standards, hardly amounting to half a tonne an acre. The farms were quite big, each man having from 1½ to 3 sections which he could work himself. Some of the farmers did not even live on their farms, but commuted daily in the busy period. Others had jobs in the towns. They were highly mechanised with some very big tackle, which was essential because of the very short growing period each summer. The farmers I met were the survivors of the streams of settlers who had invaded Western Canada from the end of the 19th century. That they, or their families, had survived was due as much to the luck which had directed them to a particular district as to anything else.

I visited another area where a friend of mine had been employed by the Government in turning resumed arable land into pasture. Resuming meant that the farmers had simply given it up and gone away. My friend Harry had some 2 million acres under his care in Saskatchewan. It had been fenced and was let for summer grazing. Some hay was made for winter feed as well. Many cereal farmers, he told me, had a few cattle, and put them out for the summer while they were cropping and took them home for the winter to eat hay and straw and grain they had harvested in the summer.

There were only two months in the year when growth could be relied on before the frosts started again. The hay they made was in the main what was called slough hay. The sloughs are depressions into which the melting snow runs, and as this evaporates the uncovered land grows heavy crops of hay. In other places they were able to let water from a stream irrigate a field and grow lucerne hay there. The hay was not made into stacks on the British pattern, but just left in untidy heaps from which it could be lifted out by tractor the following winter.

Harry took me to one township which had been completely deserted. The railway lines had been pulled up and most of the houses had been destroyed in a summer fire or hauled away for fuel, which was very scarce in those parts. Each farm had had a home on its quarter section, but of these nothing remained but the depression where each settler had dug his cellar, essential for storing vegetables through the winter and as a shelter against the occasional tornado in the summer. I thought it was a tragic place. How many lives had been disappointed when, after all the hardships of immigration – hardships indeed – the promised land turned to dust and ashes. Or more accurately to drought, crop diseases and the price slump of the 'thirties when most of the resuming happened.

Those remaining in Saskatchewan were men of substance, of course, usually the sons or grandsons of early settlers. Although times in the early 'seventies were rough, they were nothing like as bad as they had been in the pre-war days. The industrialisation of Canada provided a wonderful alternative and escape for those who would have had to leave the land anyway.

The fearful cold was something I found hard to understand, until I visited a farm where they had quite a big herd of breeding cows. The farmer was laying a water pipe and sinking it 9 ft underground to make sure it did not freeze up. Quite a few of his cows had no tails or very short ones, so I asked him why he had cut them off. He explained that in winter the cows sometimes collected icicles on their tails, and when they got heavy they were apt to break the tails off. Many of the cattle ran out all the winter and managed quite well on the standing grass which was not beaten down by the snow. The snow also provided the moisture they needed when the frost was very hard.

On only one day of our visit was there a break in the winter. We were having lunch at a ranch near the American border and during the drink session beforehand the room got very warm indeed. Our host noticed this and said this must be a chinook, a warm wind from the Pacific. A large thermometer outside the window confirmed this. He opened the windows and turned down the central heating and in the afternoon we drove round looking at the stock in our shirt sleeves.

That evening we arrived at the town of Lethbridge in southern Alberta. It was delightfully warm and Ronie insisted that I opened the bedroom window when we went to bed. At about two in the morning her teeth began to chatter, and I was driven out of bed to shut the window and turn on the central heating again. The chinook had been driven away by a cold airstream from somewhere in the frozen north which dominated the scene for the rest of our stay.

I ended up full of admiration for the courage and tenacity of the Canadian farmers. Many were deeply in debt, as were the implement agents we met in the same areas who were suffering along with the rest. They were living in modern houses and had all the home comforts except that in winter their wives and families could hardly venture out for a walk for fear of frostbite. This awful cold went on from October to about April, and even some of those who had spent their lives there were getting tired of it and talking longingly of retiring to British Columbia or California.

De-seeding pumpkins on a state farm in the Ukraine.

PART 3: TWO BRANDS OF COMMUNISM

7. To Russia – the Hard Way

My introduction to long distance journalism came quite by chance. I had been doing some desultory writing for both *Farmers Weekly* and *Farmer and Stockbreeder,* neither of which seemed to be particularly keen for me to become a regular contributor. But I persisted with perhaps one article, feature or even a letter a week, as well as some regular radio work. This was all poorly paid. The general idea seemed to be that as a prosperous farmer, which I suppose I was, I should not expect more than pocket money for what I did. But it was all good training, and I began to get adept at using the telling phrase, particularly when attacking those twin obstacles to farming progress, the National Farmers Union, and, of course, the Government of the day. My speciality, for which I was sometimes employed, was to report on farm machinery from foreign shows. This could be fun. Not so much fun was reporting British developments when individual firms showed off their wares to the Press.

After I had been pretty scathing about some developments, the pressure of advertising took command of the situation, and in the nicest possible way I was asked to no more trade shows. Trade papers are often accused of being too much under the influence of their advertisers. But in fairness to the two I knew well, their regular machinery correspondents were able to convey their opinion of a particular product in a much less hostile way than I could. Yet at the same time they put their verdict in such a way that anyone who knew the job understood exactly what they meant.

I also had a reputation as a debunker, and one afternoon in 1955, during the dead season after an early harvest, *Farmers Weekly* rang me up, and asked if I would go to the castle of some belted earl, and send up his new milk bar. This I could not do, but in desperation for something interesting to do, I asked the news editor if there was any chance of getting on a trip to Russia, which had just been organised by the old *News Chronicle* and which had an agricultural section. By a lucky chance all *Farmers Weekly's* alternative journalists had pregnant wives or were indisposed, so Geoffrey Eley welcomed the offer. It was arranged that, accompanied by photographer Gordon Craddock, I should go there with the party.

It was one thing to be issued with tickets and sufficient money, but quite another to get a Russian visa. Gordon and I spent some time in the Russian Embassy visa section, staffed by sallow young men smoking long Russian cigarettes. But we were told that although we had invitations from the Soviet Ministry of Agriculture the visa came from another department. Any approach to Russia in those days was an adventure. The Cold War was only just waning in the aftermath of Stalin's death, and my family and friends who heard about it were convinced that I would disappear into Siberia, or else be blackmailed into betraying Britain to the KGB.

Because of the uncertainty of our departure, we missed the Foreign Office lecture given in those days to those who ventured behind the Iron Curtain. According to those who did receive it, there were certain dangers in every Russian situation. At all costs intimacy with Russian women must be avoided – and with men too. Naturally all rooms and telephones were bugged, and any criticisms of our hosts should be kept to oneself, until we were clear of the frontiers. It seemed to me that, although certain individuals were likely to be at risk, because they were influential in their own countries, there were simply too many in our party to be coped with by the Russian security services, who probably knew everyone's importance to a 'T'.

Gordon and I rang the Russian Embassy every day until the time of departure. When the rest of the party had gone we decided to turn to other things. Then we were rung and told that our visas were ready, and we could go as soon as we wished. There were not jet airliners in those days, so we first flew to Oslo, then Stockholm. There we spent the night before flying on to Helsinki, a cold and desolate airfield in a cold hard country where winter had already come by the end of September. Here we met two other journalists – James Cameron and Barnet Saidman, who had left before us and were just catching the plane to Moscow.

We were not so lucky. We were told there would be no seats for three weeks and that was that. By this time it was late afternoon and there were no flights in or out of Helsinki. There were not even any hotel rooms, so we landed up in the Finnish Tourist Office, where they could or would do nothing to help us. Then I remembered my old French governess, who told me about a train which ran from Helsinki – Helsingfors in those days – to Leningrad, on which she had travelled, watched by wolves with slavering jaws. Was there still a train to Leningrad? I enquired. If so, could they get us seats on it? There was, but seats were difficult. Had we Russian visas? There was not time? Would we please go away, as it was closing time.

Here Gordon and I became obstinate. We refused to leave the office until we had a room for the night and also seats on the train. The chairs were comfortable and we had had a meal at the airport while awaiting developments there. We settled down with our paperbacks while quite urgent telephoning began. After about an hour we were handed train tickets for 9 am the next morning and given the address of a lady who would let us have a room. This was given to a taxi driver, and we set off. The room was in the flat of a lady who could have been a professor's widow. At least I guessed as much from the extensive library, all in Finnish. She showed us a little single bed in the middle of this library, but simply could not understand any European language with which I tried to communicate with her.

In the end she called up a friend on the telephone, a lady who could speak French. Through her interpretation we arranged for another bed, and the whereabouts of a restaurant. The next morning we reached the station and found we were in a very luxurious sleeping car with two berths. There was a restaurant car on the train, but on speaking to a Swedish diplomat I found that this was taken off before crossing the frontier, and there was often no food available until Moscow, some 30 hours away. 'Gordon', I said, 'this is serious. Go and find us food.' After all, I had done the lion's share of the negotiations so far. Gordon, I had discovered, was not encumbered with any language but English, and in moments of stress would revert to basics.

Later when in Moscow we had to communicate by phone with our office, I would try to charm the international operators with French, German or Spanish. To no avail. Then he would impatiently grab the phone and shout down it, 'Bloody well give me Fleet Street 5000, you stupid woman!' She invariably did this in about three minutes flat. Meanwhile I held my breath, waiting for the KGB to burst through the door. His technique as a food seeker was not so well developed, but he brought back a small cooked wild duck, some dripping and some rolls. Luckily I had a foot-rot knife in my pocket and with this we managed to tear the duck apart. It sustained us, with many glasses of tea, brought by the steward, until we crossed the frontier.

This was quite a shock. The Finnish countryside was tidy with painted houses and neat fields and small lakes and woods. The Iron Curtain was just as I had expected it to be. A long swath cut through the pine woods and Russian soldiers with high cheek bones in flat caps facing west through barbed wire. There were what looked like machine-gun posts and watch towers and on a gloomy afternoon it gave me the creeps. The first impression once over the border was of a general untidiness, unpainted log houses, each with several TV aerials on the roof. There were big fields and as we passed on I noticed about 100 women picking up potatoes, while under a tree a group of men sat playing cards. Obviously men were privileged in the Soviet Union – or was it that women had the most absolute equality? The mass employment of women was apparent everywhere, looking after herds of cows, working on the railway lines and performing the duties of signalmen, each with a small flag as the train steamed past. But this was 1955, of course, and the male population had been tragically reduced by the war. Some were in uniforms, others shawled, in drab clothing.

The first stop was Viborg, originally a Finnish town, taken in 1940 in the Russo-Finnish war. A most polite official met us, looked at our passports and told us that Intourist in Leningrad would be looking out for us. Meanwhile would we like a meal? We said we would and were led into a dining room, absolutely empty except for three buxom waitresses in white blouses standing against the wall. They simply shook their heads at his requests and went on doing so until he gave up and said there would not be time before the train left. But we could change some money and have a look at the square. He led us out of the station and there was the square – an enormous expanse with three horses and carts and nothing else in sight.

After this feast of culture we went into the bank where our guide said it would be to our advantage to change our Finnish Marks into roubles. It certainly was, because the rate we got was about 70 per cent better than we subsequently received for a straight sterling-rouble deal. Ever since then I dream I have missed a fortune in currency smuggling. The snag, as I found when I came to leave Russia later, was that the rouble was an inconvertible currency. It could not be changed back without permission and could only be exchanged for Russian goods. We reached Leningrad in darkness and Intourist found us. They supplied some very thick sandwiches filled with some black gooey substance which I eventually decided must have been caviar, and, of course, endless tea.

The Finnish passengers in our coach, some of whom spoke English, had come better prepared, and shared their vodka with us. It certainly helped the caviar down. These Finns were an extrovert lot, a party of motor agents who dealt in Russian cars. They had nothing but contempt for the Soviets. This came to a head the next day when we stopped at a station near a big aerodrome and they dashed on to the platform with their cameras photographing the Mig planes. Gordon showed signs of restlessness and wanted to get his camera out, but I had visions of diplomatic incidents, even exile to Siberia, and would not allow him to.

When I was in Leningrad I had asked the Intourist man if he knew anything about the party we were trying to join. He did say that a number had been booked into the Astoria Hotel there for the next night but he said he had had orders – whose orders, I wondered? – to send us on to Moscow. The countryside all the way was just as I always imagined Russia to be. Endless miles of pine and birch forest, villages with log houses and muddy roads and a generally shabby ambience. The cultivated fields did not look much better. There were still troops guarding bridges and on the platforms of the stations we passed great crowds of people waiting for trains.

Some Russians joined the train at Leningrad. According to the Finns one was a top general. Once on the move they changed into pyjamas and some of them socialised in the corridors. I suppose Gordon and I looked English, because quite a few tried out their English on us and several said they used the language to study technical publications and listen to either the BBC or Voice of America. Did I know either of these two organisations, I was asked. I thought this was extraordinary. I had been so brainwashed by the tales of Soviet oppression and the jamming of Western radio that I thought listening to them and even admitting it would be dangerous. Perhaps these people were agents provocateurs, trying to trap us into some dangerous situation?

This feeling lasted a long time during my stay and almost became a certainty when in Kiev Cathedral, I was approached by a sallow youth in cap and threadbare suit and asked in very good English indeed if I could whistle for him the last four bars of 'Kiss of Fire'! I had just no idea at all what this meant. But the more I denied all knowledge of it, the more he began to whistle. Obviously some code. Perhaps some other member of the party was in fact an agent. At length I was made to understand. 'Kiss of Fire' was the title of a popular song which had been the rage on Voice of America. This young man's group had transposed it for their own use in a jazz band they had formed, but had got the ending wrong and the Americans had not played it lately. We became quite friendly after that. It turned out that he was a teacher of English and had been taught by a man who had never seen an English-speaking person nor had this man's instructor. They were encouraged, they told me, to listen to the two radio stations. It appeared that only the Russian language broadcasts were jammed. The rest were a source of such Western culture as jazz music, as well as coloquial English. In fact, most hotels we stayed in, and the one night club we went to, had small orchestras grinding out such classics as 'Red Sails in the Sunset' and 'Smoke Gets in Your Eyes'.

When we reached Moscow, another Intourist man knew just where to find us, put us in an enormous Buick-type limousine and took us swiftly past great crowds of pedestrians, all walking along with their eyes on the ground and without a smile on their faces. The Muscovites looked strained and worried, the only place in Russia where I got this feeling. But I guessed in the end that the population was at the centre of things and were busily making their way in the Communist bureaucracy, which was as much a rat-race as anywhere in the capitalist West. You see the same sort of thing in the City of London and in New York.

The National Hotel, where the Press were lodged, had a policeman at the door and a lift which was nearly always out of order. Our passports were taken, and we were shown into a room furnished in the most elaborate Victorian style with heavy curtains and carpet-like tablecloths, and a bathroom where during our stay there was no hot water and no plugs in bath or basin. Once installed and after ordering two beers, which we discovered cost £1 each even in those days, I set to work to find the rest of our party. Who would be better to guide me than the British Embassy? In the Intourist office I found an English-speaking girl who put me through. A very refined voice answered my query with the information that the rest of the party had departed for Soviet Asia that morning. But they had heard about us and would contact us when they had any news. Meanwhile we were advised not to leave the hotel without our passports. The Embassy would be closed until Monday. (It was then Friday.)

This was discouraging. I began to regret my persistence and wished that we had stayed and done some sort of a story in Scandinavia. Then, turning round, I saw Jim Muir from Rothamsted Experimental Station, who I knew to be on the trip. It was quite true, he told me, that some people had gone off to the east, but the rest were still in Moscow, though his own party of scientists was leaving for Leningrad that night. The whole thing was being organised from room 916 of the Moskva Hotel across the square. He took us over there, showed us into the room and left us.

For a long time Gordon and I did nothing but sit and smile politely at the three Russian occupants, who with short haircuts and Slav features looked just like a KGB team I had seen on the films. Then a young woman came in and spoke to us in English.

I explained my position, that we had been invited to Moscow to report on their farming, and not only was I with the leading farming magazine but also contributed to *The Times* of London. Gordon and I had been sent to Russia at great expense and did not wish to remain immured in the National Hotel until the time came for us to leave. After she had put our case there was a long silence. Then one of the Russians made a short statement. It was impossible, she told me. Jim Muir's party was leaving that evening for Leningrad, there were no berths on the train, there were no seats on the planes we were going to use to travel the country, there was no room in the hotels. We would have to stay in Moscow and the Ministry of Agriculture would look after us the next week when we had got our passports back again. And she made to leave us.

This was the time for desperate measures. I seized her arm and implored her to put our case for joining the party once more. I exaggerated the power and influence I had over the content of the British Press, to say nothing of the BBC. We had the money to support ourselves, we would travel hard to Leningrad again and would sleep in hotel lounges if there were no rooms. She kept trying to get away but I had a tight grip. Then she re-addressed the Russians. If ever I look like falling for some Russian woman, shoot me first. She belted at them in what must have been the most emotional Russian terms, or perhaps my grip was hurting. They looked shiftily away from me while it went on and on for the best part of a quarter of an hour. Then she stopped. One of the Russians said something to her and she asked me if we had any English coins and stamps. Gordon and I turned out our pockets. The Russians gathered round and made a selection. Then the most senior man, whom I later discovered to have been the Minister of Agriculture for the Federal Republic, made a short speech welcoming me to the party. The sleepers were booked for us, our hotels and plane tickets were available and our passports would be handed to us when we left the hotel.

It was a marvellous deliverance and the catalyst was Luba Yurieva, who remained with us as interpreter. A young woman of incredible stamina who translated everything that came between us and Russian understanding at all hours of the day and night. Long official speeches, technical discussions between scientists, and simple requests like mine for a gargle for the sore throat I had developed. This she duly provided and I poured it into a glass of water. It frothed there and I took a big mouthful. It kept on frothing and was certainly a shampoo. Was it a translation error, a piece of Russian mislabelling? We shall never know. But Gordon asked me if the information I had gained through her was accurate. A good question. So with that in mind, my first account of Russian farming should be taken at its face value!

The hardships of a foreign correspondent: breakfast in a Moscow hotel.

8. Russian Farming and the People

My visit to Russia coincided with a momentous change in that country's affairs. Stalin had just been debunked by Kruschev and among the objects of Kruschev's scorn was the work of the scientist Lysenko. He first came to fame as a breeder or selector of wheats which by the process of vernalisation – exposing the seeds to low temperatures so they germinated more promptly – he had successfully grown several hundred miles further north than had been done before.

If he had stuck to his work on vernalisation, which he applied to other plants as well, Lysenko would doubtless have gone down in history as one of the great pioneers. But unfortunately he got carried away with various theories. What was even more unfortunate, he had Stalin's backing. It was unfortunate both for the Russians and for any scientists who disagreed with him, because they were silenced as only Stalin knew how to do. The whole affair was really a confrontation between the Darwinian theory of evolution through natural selection, and Lysenko's, which was that acquired characteristics could be inherited. A common example was that if a tree was naturally bent by the wind, the seed of that tree would produce a tree that would be bent in the same way.

When this was thoroughly debunked, as it would be by Western scientists, he propounded the cluster theory. Briefly this was that one sowed seeds of fruits, cereals or trees in clusters. This cluster would grow and eventually the dominant plants would emerge and outyield all the others. When I was on a farm near Odessa they were planting not only potatoes but also oak trees on this principle. When I asked how long it would be before the results showed up in the oak trees, I was told that it would be at least 300 years. When I suggested that the result would be just the opposite with the resulting trees forming a stunted clump they just shook their heads. On this farm the debunking of Lysenko had obviously not reached the management because in a glass case in the entry hall there was a pokerwork chess box with the outlines of Stalin and Lysenko on the lid. They were smoking, and the smoke mingled above their heads.

In other areas practices were much more normal and the scientists we met – I was with a party of scientists – were every bit as well informed as ours. They already had the knowledge to grow all the food the Soviets might need, or could, with their contacts with the scientific West, have very soon done so. In Leningrad we visited the plant breeding institute where they maintain viable stocks of all the seeds used throughout the world. The livestock institutes we saw also had all the knowledge essential for farming progress and all the breeds common in the West are found there too.

But, and it is a big but, the systems of farming practised in the field seemed to be very different indeed from what we saw in the research stations. Somewhere down the chain of command the knowledge got mislaid or was not applied. Part of the problem lay in the system itself. The farms were of two kinds – state farms directly run by the State and Kholkoz's, best described as cooperatives or collectives. The striking feature of both systems was the enormous amount of labour employed. It is true that in China there are even bigger numbers on the land but then they have no mechanisation and indeed the systems of double cropping employed mean that mechanisation is out. But in Russia there was plenty of mechanisation. One of the first things we were shown when we visited a farm was the machinery park. State farms had their own machines but the collectives had to make use of the machinery stations from which tractors and other machines were hired out.

A peculiar feature was the task work, or norm. Everyone had to do so much work for a given reward, usually paid in cash and kind. They were called day work tasks, but the work done bore no relation, in my eyes, to a true day's work. For instance, one old lady was topping and tailing turnips and had a pile which had been measured out for her by the foreman. It would have weighed about a tonne and any active man or woman on my farm, in the days when we used to grow turnips, could have done the job in about half an hour. She told us herself she usually took a couple of hours and did three or four such heaps in the day. I came to the conclusion that setting the rewards was a racket. All farm work was paid for on this basis, as indeed was work in many other fields. The object was to set the task as low as possible, so the manager could report to headquarters that his staff had done so many days work and he would get added kudos himself and probably a bonus as well.

We did not see much of the famous private plots which are supposed to be the basis of much of Russian food supplies to the exclusion of the official farming. But we did see in country districts that every lorry carried as part of its load a number of women off to town with market baskets. In fact, the train on which we travelled to Moscow stopped at one station where a crowd of women swarmed on the platform selling to the passengers cans of milk which we understood to be the product of private cows. If they were, there were a lot of them because just outside the station several women were milking quite a sizable herd! This probably accounted for the very low yields of Russian cows, the lowest of any country that produces statistics. I don't think this had anything to do with the systems of farming though, but simply that much production was diverted into private hands. This was undoubtedly going on then and is most probably going on now.

One example of the task work system affected silage making. It was October and all over Russia they were making maize silage. Very green and wet in the North and very dry in the South. Each team had transport tractors, lorries, bullocks or horses. Every load had to be weighed between the field and the pit so that work could be paid for. This resulted in some of the transport having to make a very long trip indeed between the field, the weighbridge and the silage pit. This must have added enormously to the cost and the time of operation, especially when bullocks were used.

We spent some time on a state farm outside Leningrad. In fact, it had been inside the Russian lines during the siege of the city and the chairman had been in charge then. He told us that they kept up their production all through the siege and lost many of the workers when they were in the fields from shellfire. But he claimed they never stopped production. When we were there it was a wet and muddy place, just getting ready for the winter and no fun to farm under shellfire or at any other time. They had quite a good herd of Holstein cows but their milk yields were so low that we thought either they did not get enough to eat or some of the milk was siphoned off.

Near Kiev though, things looked much better. The land is a wonderful loam or brick earth many feet deep, the young wheat, which we were told had only been in a fortnight, was already well up in the drills, and all looked set for a really good harvest. Yet the expected yields were very low indeed and depended on the winter snows. If there was no snow the frost could kill the wheat. If it did not there would be no moisture for the summer. This particular farm had a big herd of pigs and each of the girls who looked after them was responsible for three sows and lived in a little room close to the farrowing pens. Once farrowed every sow had her teats numbered. The little pigs were numbered to match and each made to keep to its own teat.

We asked to see the workers' houses and were taken at random into one on the side of the road. It was clean inside but very basic as to furnishings. We had a trade unionist in the party who was very anxious to know about the sanitary arrangements for the workers. So we asked the lady of the house where her privy was. With a gesture she opened the door and pointed to the steppes outside! What did intrigue us was the fact that there was only one bed, and that a single one, so we asked where they slept. They pointed to the big stove across one end of the room and said it was best there in the winter and on the floor in the summer.

While in Kiev we had a meeting with the Minister of Agriculture for the Ukraine and I asked him when they were going to start exporting cereals to the world again. I reminded him that on the outbreak of the First World War in 1914 some 370 grain ships were marooned in the Black Sea due to the closure of the Dardanelles. He replied that he could tell me nothing about this but he thought that there would be a good market for all they produced within Russia.

There was a sequel to this a little later. When we reached Moscow there was a cable from *Farmers' Weekly* asking me to follow up 'quickest' the story on Russian barley exports. The last place to find out anything of what was going on in Russia was certainly in the country itself. I rang the Ministry of Agriculture and the British Embassy, both of whom were unwilling to talk, and it was not until I came home that I found out what had happened. Apparently the Russians had dumped cargoes of barley on the market without warning and at a very low price and during the succeeding period of low prices had purchased some million tonnes until the Western merchants woke up to the trick. For all their hostility against capitalism, the Communists can perform very well in the markets when they put their minds to it, as the Great Grain Robbery of the US stockpile demonstrated years later. I was involved in the latter event to the extent that I had advance information of it but never made use of it for profit or for journalism. In 1974 the commodities office of the *Financial Times* was rung up from somewhere in the US and told by someone who refused to divulge his name or status that the Russians were buying the American stockpile. I was asked to try and find out about it but learnt nothing from our usual sources who professed ignorance. I believe they *were* ignorant, though they should not have been.

Battling with bureaucracy: Luba, with her back to the camera, trying to get my passport back.

Weighing loads of silage on a Russian collective farm (Kholkoz).

Parties always started well.

Looking at Simmenthal cattle in the Ukraine (the author is second from right).

We suggested to the Editor that we should publish something about it but he refused, saying that we must get confirmation which neither we nor our staff in the US could do. Who our informant was I have no idea – probably some disgruntled employee in an international grain trader's office. Anyway we missed the scoop of a lifetime.

What did surprise me was that during my many miles of travel both in the Ukraine and then by the Black Sea I never saw any grain silos nor were there any on the farms. Subsequent travellers have told me that they saw none either, so I can only conclude that all the grain is buried underground or else shipped off to Moscow.

What did stand out a mile was that there was a wide gulf between the administrators and the men on the farms. The former were probably Party members or professional bureaucrats, while the men and women actually doing the work probably had a very much better idea of what was going on.

One of the features of the Russian excursion was the party-giving everywhere we went. Unlike China, where for the most part the refreshment was tea in great and lukewarm quantities, the Russians went in for the hard stuff, together with lots and lots of lovely caviar. The hard stuff was vodka – a drink I have never taken since – and in Russia served neat and taken at a gulp. I can truthfully say that although I kept my end up in the incessant toasts I was never put under the table as many of my hosts and companions were.

In spite of legends to the contrary, the Russians do not have cast iron heads. They enjoy the party spirit and react to it in the usual way. I was fortunate in that, because I was not a leader of the party, I was able now and then to substitute mineral water for vodka in my glass. I did this when I began to lose count of my toes. Losing count of one's toes is as good a way of telling one is going over the limit as any I know. So I was able to respond to all the toasts with enthusiasm!

I generally tried to sit next to a Russian who spoke English or another European language. Some of them spoke some German and in this way gave a different slant on the situation from that given by the official interpreter. At one party I sat next to the director of an animal breeding institute, who told me a good deal of the difficulties and shortages of resources which were affecting his work. He was particularly angry about the inefficiency of the local bosses who held their positions through rewards from the Party or for war service. Science, he said, should never have a master, but he had too many and they knew nothing.

As the vodka flowed he grew more and more expansive. I did not ask him if he was a Communist as our conversation in broken German was being increasingly followed by an individual across the table, a great bull of a man, who introduced himself as the potato boss of the Ukraine. The director and I got friendly exchanging details of our families and so on and I said I hoped to see him if ever he came to England, as he might well do in his position. A few days later I was waiting in Moscow airport for the flight home when I met him again. He refused to recognise me, and walked off, obviously very embarrassed.

The potato boss told me that in the war he had ridden from Stalingrad to Berlin on the same horse, that he enjoyed Russian women, big women, 100 kilo women, and after experiencing all the women of Eastern Europe he could find nothing better. He did not want to talk about his work, and his German was so bad that if he had been following my previous conversation he would not have been much the wiser.

After the first few days I did not get the feeling that everything we were doing was being watched and that our conversations in English were being monitored. Frankly, we weren't influential enough to engage the resources of the KGB. You have to remember that at that time the Russians were said to be planning our downfall. It was only when I got there that I found that the average Russian thought exactly the same about the West, particularly the Americans. Really the situation was one of profound ignorance on both sides. Russian diplomats and journalists reported back to their masters in terms that they thought fitted with Communist beliefs, and I believe most Western reporters and diplomats tended to do the same. They probably still do. This is a great pity because many of the Russians we met were easy to get on with and the Russian politician type and Party boss at the local level were very like their British and American counterparts. Not particularly valuable members of the human race in ethical terms, but essential to the running of any society.

As an indication of the degree to which propaganda was always surfacing, I was accused by Bogorelov, the Minister accompanying the party, that when he had been in England some months before he had only been shown the very best of everything. I asked him where he had gone, and he said it was by train to Scotland, and he had been particularly impressed by Wigan where he had spent a night. At that time Wigan Pier was a bad joke in England and I said we had many much better areas. He would not believe me. This man tried to make me drink half a tumbler of neat vodka before breakfast. At the risk of causing an international incident I refused and handed it back to him explaining through Luba, our interpreter, that I had a disability which made this sort of refreshment impossible before midday.

He also professed to be very shocked by the number of couples he had seen making love in London parks. It would never happen in Russia. I suppose it is too cold in Russia for the same behaviour. Soon after that we were in Odessa, and outside our hotel was a park where in the moonlight numbers of couples were inextricably entwined on the grass and on the seats. In triumph I returned to the hotel, dragged Bogorelov and Luba outside and showed them what I had seen. I asked for their comments. 'You must remember, Mr Cherrington,' Luba said most demurely, 'that Odessa is a port. It must be the influence of foreign sailors.'

There was a good deal of talk in those days of diplomats and others being blackmailed through having been compromised by women, or even men. From my observations very few Russian women were beautiful enough to seduce anyone. Perhaps the best had been retained for the more important travellers! The most beautiful girl I did meet was the friend of a young lawyer who had been attached to us to improve her English – or so he said. She was good looking and wore her clothes with real style. I asked her what she did, and she told me she was a metallurgical engineer.

My overall impression at the time, both of the farming and of everything else, was of supreme inefficiency by Western standards. I don't know whether this is a Communist or a Russian characteristic. I suspect a good deal of the latter. It should be remembered though that the country had passed through 40 years of war and revolution and that the losses of able people in both wars and the revolutions had been immense. As had been the destruction. Farming also suffers from a climate which is far from easy, though no worse than the Canadians and some of the Americans have to deal with. The capitalist system has been shown to be more efficient in production. But again I am not sure that this is not because the Western European nations found themselves well adapted to modern industrial techniques.

What the Russians have managed to do, by their own account, is to provide full employment for everyone, which the West seems unable to do these days. Though Communism is not very attractive as a 'religion', which indeed it is, if it delivers what people consider a better life, it will become increasingly attractive to those who feel deprived of the means of living through the capitalist inefficiency of slump and unemployment.

9. China – the Task of Providing for All

When I was in Russia many years ago, I was sitting in a Moscow night club with our party's interpreters, watching quite a good display of conjuring, and drinking vodka. Our male interpreter was remarking on the number of Chinese in the audience, members of delegations and others, privileged to enjoy the delights, such as they were, of Moscow's night life. 'What', I asked him, 'do you think of the Chinese, who you seem to be cultivating so assiduously? Are you not fearful that one of these days they will turn on you, and then twice 700 million feet will come pattering westwards over the steppes? It will be no good looking to the West for support. You will be on your own then.' 'Do you really think so, Mr Cherrington?' he said. 'Yes. Think of Genghis Khan and Tamerlane. It is part of the inexorable logic of history.'

Since then Chinese numbers have increased. There are now 1,000 million of them and the Russians are worried sick. So would I be if I had some thousands of miles of common frontier with them. Not that they are looking particularly warlike. Beyond rather shabbily dressed soldiers on bridges and such places you don't see many signs of militarism in China. But you do see a *lot* of people! This was the first and most striking impression I had after landing at Peking airport, and on travels throughout the country. There were swarms of them. All dressed more or less alike, all very ready to smile – or is it to laugh? – at the West. Unlike most Asian and African countries there are no beggars, no rags and no bare footed people, except in the paddy fields.

In three weeks it is impossible to see more than a fraction of the country, but in that time the party I was with spent three days in trains, steam trains for the most part, and in buses, and travelled a very great distance. Our main purpose, of course, was to see the farming, and as a farmer I was most impressed. Not in terms of the actual systems but with the overall success of Chinese farming in feeding so many mouths. Statistically the Chinese have to feed 11 people, and clothe them too, on each hectare of arable land – just over four to the acre. This is a stupendous achievement in a country as diverse as this, with much of the cultivated land in northern latitudes.

In all our journeys we saw very few neglected crops. Where they were poor it was through lack of moisture, failures of irrigation or shortages of fertilisers. There is no shortage of manpower, or of womanpower either. The fields were crowded with people, but they were working intelligently, making the best of what they had. The Chinese seem to have an innate knowledge of how to grow things and the farmers in our party could appreciate this.

The first sight I had of the farming was from the air when flying into Peking. I could not identify the crops, because the fields were divided into plots with paths between them. On closer acquaintance I found the crop was wheat and the spaces between the plots were seed beds for other crops – maize, cotton, soya beans, and so on, with which the wheat is interplanted. About a month before harvest the growing plants are replanted among the standing wheat. Then the wheat is harvested almost green on the straw. It is taken to a threshing floor where it is allowed to dry before being thrashed out with a flail or with some primitive machine or even rolled out with rollers. These beaten clay thrashing floors are everywhere.

This double cropping was general around Peking, but as we went south, rice was brought into the programme where possible. The most intensive system we saw was a rotation of one wheat crop followed by two rice crops in the same year. I was told that if the second rice harvest was delayed that wheat was sprouted in a glasshouse and then planted out. Because of this double cropping, Chinese yields have to be highly qualified. Officials will tell you that they harvest between three and six tonnes an acre. But when this figure is examined all the crops grown are calculated down to a cereal equivalent. Even potatoes are included. I quite believed them when they said that their winter wheat averaged about two tonnes an acre, to which in the course of the year they added beans, potatoes, maize and so on.

This system requires an enormous labour force, of course. But then some 70 per cent of the population is on the land. Land work is not too popular with what we might call the intellectuals. One of our interpreters told us she had been sent from university to work on a farm for a time during the Cultural Revolution. I don't believe all these people were needed to work the system, but the country was a good place to send the excess urban population. Living conditions were very basic everywhere. Even the workers' show houses were barely furnished with few possessions. We were told that many of the houses on the communes belonged to the workers or members and that on some communes they could have plots for themselves. We saw some of these, and they were as well cultivated as one could expect. They could also keep hens or a pig.

There are 20,000 communes in the country, but these are only loosely based on farming. Rather they form what could be termed regional administration centres which include farming but also factories and all sorts of other activities. The farms are run by special production brigades and the other activities have their own organisations too. This whole organisation developed after Mao and his supporters took over the administration of the country in 1949, when the Nationalists were driven out. They formed co-operatives to begin with, but eventually these were brought under closer State control as the Communist Party consolidated its power.

I am far from being a Communist, but there seemed to be no alternative to Communism for China at that time. The country had been ravaged by some 30 years of civil war, culminating in the Japanese invasion and the corruption of the Chiang Kai-Shek regime. People we spoke to, admittedly through interpreters, were thankful that the Communists had prevented starvation and replaced anarchy with security. This has been enough for 30 years. But now it appears there are those who think there should be other political alternatives. So, forgetting hunger, the Chinese will no doubt try to find some way out of the drab existence most of them have to endure.

This is just what one would expect, and the fact that these sentiments have erupted, points to the Communists' success in establishing order out of chaos. The Chinese now have other things than the next meal to think of. Their progress would have come sooner had not the so called Gang of Four, led by Mao's widow, instituted a reign of terror against all forms of progress, apparently trying to force the people back to the absolute fundamentals of Marxist theory. The Chinese still talked to us about it in hushed tones. No doubt when it was going on they had to keep their heads down and hope for the best.

Even so they have done better than any other Third World country I have seen in securing at least a measure of security and human dignity for their inhabitants. For those hundreds of millions in South America, Africa and Asia who live in destitution and squalor I would have thought a Chinese solution could be a first step towards getting a better deal. After all, mankind is mainly interested in enough food, clothing and shelter. Any society which cannot provide these basics for a start is at risk from systems like the Chinese.

The Chinese are fortunate in their soils. Much of it is loess, a fertile top soil originally blown from the Gobi Desert. When it settled in Central China it formed a soft rock which can be easily worked and tilled to form a good friable mineral soil which will grow anything when properly handled. On one commune we saw dwellings cut into the loess cliffs, bricks made from it, and terraces cut by hand from the hills so that irrigation water can be applied. Any of the water that is not absorbed by the crops filters through the soil and can be used again. In some parts the terracing has to be seen to be believed. It looks as though some giant has been carving the country up into squares and rectangles. Plenty of water is available in the big rivers, and now they have controlled the Yellow River by shifting its course several score miles northward, the floods that used to bring destruction and famine are no longer a regular occurrence.

The terracing, and in fact the whole farming operation, has been done by hand by thousands of men and women cutting out the soil and transporting it in baskets and barrows for quite long distances. A great deal of the transport everywhere depends on human muscles. In every town there are long processions of barrows, carts and rickshaws transporting anything from night soil to coal, gravel and vegetables. There are horses as well as bullocks for the heavier loads, but lorries are few and far between. By Western European standards this is a dreadful misuse of human resources, brutal work that could easily be done by machine. But then the people are there, they have to be employed, and there is no other employment for most of them.

In the streets of Sian, the ancient capital, there were little benches with old people selling tea and mineral water. Was this, I asked, a form of private industry, free enterprise? Nothing of the sort. Those who kept these stalls were older members of some commune or other, earning a little more to help pay their old age pensions. No one would be allowed to starve, but on the other hand, no one was allowed to be idle as long as he was able to do something. Being a grandfather myself I would not care to be one in China. We visited a neighbourhood committee in Peking (a sort of administrative part of the local authority). Grandparents, we were told, looked after the family while the younger couples went to work. In fact, they were an essential part of the family set-up.

They did not have many children to look after. The ideal number of children is only one, and marriage is not encouraged before the age of 25 or so. Birth control is free on demand, and sex is taboo. There is none of the pornography, the obsession with sex, which is so prevalent in Western society these days. No pin-ups and no girlie magazines. We asked our interpreter how in practice it was possible to prevent sex rearing its ugly head, as it does everywhere else in the world. What happens if boy meets girl, and takes her for a walk? The mother talks to us both, he said with feeling.

Of course, the communes we were taken to see, and the houses we visited, were hand-picked, as they would have been anywhere else in the world. We did not have a chance to look into the real workings of anything, and not having the language we could not anyway. But the Chinese seemed to be pleased to see us, if only because when we were there they had the chance to join a party. I am sure there is real injustice in the workings of many communes and factories. The Chairmen or bosses had the look of political bosses or trade union leaders in any other part of the world.

We stayed two nights in Da Chai, a famous place in the China of Mao's day, but now losing some of its reputation. It was the model farm for the whole country. Everywhere walls and mountainsides were engraved with the characters saying 'Look to Da Chai'. It was originally a village on the side of a hill with three steep ravines in it. The loess soil was particularly subject to erosion and the village's history, as we were told it, was mainly one of floods, starvation, exploitation by the landlord class and Japanese invasion. All undoubtedly true of the China of that time. After 1949 Da Chai became a co-operative. One of the leaders was a guerrilla fighter who fought the Japanese and at the same time had the welfare of farming at heart. He must also have been a man of considerable propagandising ability, because he persuaded the State and eventually Mao to support the development of his village into a model farm. Only in this way could adequate resources be found.

The hills and ravines were terraced, irrigation was installed, there was considerable tree planting, and production increased dramatically, admittedly from a very low base. One of the newer developments was spray as opposed to flood irrigation, a move which would dramatically increase the efficiency of irrigation over that done by traditional methods and make less terracing necessary.

We stayed in the hostel attached to the village and shall never forget it. The beds were no more than shelves with a thin blanket on which I twisted and turned for two whole nights. Waking early, though not from sleep, I

The Great Wall of China.

Building new terraces in Da Chai.

The terrace system at Da Chai.

Mechanised rice planting at Shanghai.

looked out of the window and saw bus-loads of Chinese being marshalled to inspect the farm. This was about 5.30 am. Later that day we came across them in the fields taking notes and photographs. They were leaders of other farm communes who had come to learn the Da Chai methods. There were over 1,000 there that day, and we were told that up to half a million visitors from China went to Da Chai every year, besides those from overseas, usually Third World countries.

During the last year there have been big changes in China. The former leadership has been attacked, including much of Mao's reputation. Da Chai is now being vilified for not having told the truth about its results and its costs. The only thing I have to say about this is that most demonstration farms I have come across in various countries, a good deal more sophisticated than China in the '70s, are not above falsifying their results to make a better showing or to support their ideas. I thought that those running Da Chai were doing a good job showing the Chinese just how it was possible to turn three ravines in a sand mountain to productive farming. The cost in financial terms and in human terms too was doubtless very heavy. They were still building terraces by hand when we were there, as they were all over China. But the methods taught were basically sound. Nothing of the enforced adoption of Lysenko's teachings as in Russia under Stalin.

Nor did we see anything that might be construed as a sign of oppression. The police, mainly used on traffic duty, were not armed. There were soldiers, but they looked to me like Chinese in uniform with little or no badges of rank. They were little in evidence in the cities, though we passed a few camps in the country. The enormous crowds we saw in all the streets seemed to be well disciplined and good humoured. This makes their behaviour during such episodes as the Cultural Revolution difficult to understand. Under the pressure of propaganda these seemingly quiet good-humoured crowds simply turned into mobs prepared to tear down all previous authority under the instigation of the so-called Gang of Four. Even children in schools turned against their teachers so that all, or nearly all, intellectual progress in China ceased for some years.

I asked one of our interpreters what the Gang of Four were really after. Power, he said, just power. They had lost out and wanted to get back again. How this was going to happen once the whole country had descended into the abyss of anarchy is not clear. Perhaps they really thought the Chinese people would turn to them in the hope that they could restore some form of order out of chaos. These, of course, are terrorist tactics used the world over. Occasionally they succeed. But pitching China back into anarchy so soon after Mao had rescued them from it was a pretty wrong-headed proposition on the part of the Gang. But then any extremist sect, whether monetarists, Marxists or others in between, is characterised by an intolerance of the human factor and an ignorance of human nature. It's probably a safeguard against the permanent exercise of authority. Dictatorships contain the seeds of their own destruction.

We were continually amazed by the great crowds in the streets. Were these people all out of work, we asked, or was it a weekly holiday? It appeared that one seventh of the population was on holiday every day, with the other six sevenths at work. If this was true, it is obvious there would be no room for anyone to move if they all had the day off together. These crowds were everywhere, particularly on the Great Wall, the various palaces, and so on. Talking to them through the interpreters, it appeared that many had travelled from all over China just to have a look at these memorials of the past. Foreign visitors were very much in a minority.

Although the adults were drably dressed, the children were very colourful and looked well fed and happy. So much so that at one kindergarten we visited one of our farmers asked how much milk they were given. 'Milk?' said the head of the school. 'Haven't you heard of cholesterol in the West? Here we give them bean curds.' They certainly seemed to thrive on them. The fine healthy children certainly weren't confined to a few selected kindergartens for Westerners to visit. One saw them everywhere walking in crocodiles with their teachers. Not only in Peking but in the other cities as well. On the farms too the children looked very well. The women were all dressed in the same style of tunic and trousers as the men. There was very little colour in their dress. Some had different coloured blouses. In the south with their jackets off they did show a splash of individuality. But only in Hong Kong did I see just how lovely young Chinese girls could be. Whether this modesty was directed from above as part of the move to limit the population, or whether it is innate in the Chinese character, I don't know.

In the trains we travelled in Western-style sleeping cars, with full length berths, a legacy of the Russians, I gathered. These were not air-conditioned, and it was impossible to keep the windows open because of the smuts from the coal-burning locomotives. The only thing we had was a fan in the roof and this took to failing in the hottest part of the night. I went to find the conductor of our carriage, a Chinese girl who looked about 14 but was probably twice that age. I made signs that the fan had stopped, so she took me to her control booth where she put back the switch which had fallen out of its clip. After another half-hour's sleep it stopped again and I went along to find her. She was not there, so I put the switch back and went to bed again. It failed again and I thought this is too easy and went to her booth. But she came in just when I was putting it back. She got very angry, pushed me out, locked the door and disappeared up the train. I dug out our interpreter, Mr Wu and asked him to find her and get us some fresh air. He had no success. She refused to open her booth and said that the fan needed its rest just as much as any Westerner and should be left in peace. No doubt it was a demarcation dispute of some sort!

I was most impressed by the crowds at the stations. They queued in long lines in the concourses outside, and the platforms were usually empty except when a train was in. When our train stopped at stations, crowds of Chinese came on to the platform from the carriages into which they had been crowded and washed themselves thoroughly at open ablution blocks on the platforms. We had to make do in tiny loos on the train itself, which were impossible for the average well-built man to get into.

Though ample, the food was not very good. Not as good, at least, as the sort of Chinese food one gets in the West. But then Western Chinese food is what the Chinese who went to Malaysia used to cook for their European masters. We had one or two memorable meals but for the most part it was pretty ordinary. But then Chinese cooking is generally speaking that of a poor country where the inhabitants make do, or make the best, of what there is. If you have a good sauce and a few bean shoots and rice you can turn almost anything into a fairly tasty dish.

Where I do think they failed was with the tea. There were huge thermos flasks everywhere. In the bedrooms and railway carriages, and at meetings. The tea was a very dull flaky leaf, usually green. As the water was never boiling the infusion was very half-hearted but I was very thirsty and had been told that no water was safe to drink unless it had been boiled. But I was none too sure of the safety of tea after seeing the maid at one hotel fill the thermos from the hot tap.

We saw some very good concerts and circuses but here another Chinese peculiarity came to light. The audience would clap the artist as he or she came on to the stage, listen quietly through the performance, and then let him finish, bow to the audience and walk off in dead silence. We were shown quite a bit of industry too, from the Shanghai tractor factory to some quite sophisticated lathe-making plants on communes. All were characterised by a lack of organisation and industrial discipline, with dirt and rusty components everywhere. It would be some time, we thought, before the Chinese could overtake the Japanese, or even the Europeans. In spite of this apparent inefficiency, some of the machine shops on the country communes were turning out some fairly good machine tools. No doubt in a state of war these scattered workshops could make rifles, guns and bombs as well as anywhere.

When I was there the Western nations were falling over themselves to sell high technology and almost everything else to the Chinese. There were trade missions in all the hotels where we stayed. But I couldn't see where the Chinese were going to get the money from to pay for these things. I was taken to meet the Vice-Minister of Foreign Trade and asked him if he was going to buy British tractors. 'Of course, not in any quantity', he said. 'We will buy one or two and then manufacture them here under licence and pay some royalties'. Now the Chinese have cancelled many of their contracts with the West and Japan, as it was obvious they were going to have to do.

Ploughing for rice – Canton.

PART 4: POLITICS AND EUROPE

10. European Farming – Still Based on the Small Unit

During 1962 I was invited by the BBC to help make a film about farming. The reason for this was the Government's decision to request membership of the EEC. Agriculture featured prominently in all accounts of the Community, so more ought to be known about it. The general impression at that time, in British eyes at least, was that while British farming was a most efficient and streamlined industry, it was nothing like so advanced in the rest of Europe. The general view was that, with the exception of Danish bacon and Dutch horticulture, European farmers were peasants, milking a couple of cows on some mountain slopes – very much in need of the stimulus that British farmers, slimmed down by long years of depression, could give them by their competitiveness. They could not have been more wrong.

It was and is quite true that because of the Enclosure Acts and economic pressures, Britain is by and large a country of larger farms than those in Europe. European farms are generally smaller because at the time the Enclosure Acts were driving the once free British peasants out of the country and into the town, the Europeans, dominated by Napoleon, brought in a measure, the Code Napoléon, which still applies for the most part. This lays down that when a man dies his property is divided equally between his children. This was the complete antithesis of the primogeniture that kept British farming and other property in very few hands – the eldest sons of the eldest sons, in fact. In Europe it meant that farms got smaller and smaller as succeeding generations divided the loot on the death of their fathers.

This led to an absurd fragmentation of holdings in many European countries. Yet everyone had an interest in keeping this law. The eldest son usually secured the farmsteading and a little land, and then had to buy out those of his siblings he could persuade to sell their land. Or he could rent it off them. This means that in practice a large proportion of the population, particularly in France and Germany, have an interest in the land and in farming. Over half the land in France is tenanted and the number of those interested, because their holdings are very small, swells the farming vote enormously. Therefore all European governments, while paying lip service to the modernisation of farms and the need to become competitive, support their farmers in ways that no British Government has ever done.

In Bavaria I saw farms which had been fragmented to an enormous extent by constant sub-division. One man had 20 acres (8.1 hectares) made up of 50 different plots, some of them seven miles (11 km) apart. This confusion of land holdings was widely deplored, and the German Government was trying to amalgamate them into more manageable units. This was difficult. The plots were so scattered because the land had come into the family through marriage, and when holdings were divided every account had to be taken of the quality of the land. 'Everyone knows', one farmer told me, 'that the land the other side of the trees is not as good as it is here. Why should I have to give up this and make do with what are the worst fields in the parish?'

I had gone out with the same man to spray some barley some five miles from his steading. His plot was in a line of other plots, each about 15 yd (13.7 m) by 60 yd (54.8 m) with no distinguishing mark. He counted them off the headland, made a mistake, and in the end sprayed two more to be sure. Nevertheless, he told me, he was going to agree to the re-organisation of his holding, so it would be in two fields within a short distance of his house. The Government was going to build a new steading and pay all the costs of moving and so on. The whole exercise would cost a good deal more than the price of a decent farm in Britain at the time.

The German Government was not content with spending vast sums on restructuring farms. There was a determined policy to take industry to the countryside, so that farmers, and their families, would not have to leave home to work, but could maintain the rural way of life by working part time in factories. The programme was most successful and a very large proportion of German farmers, particularly in Bavaria and central and southern Germany, are part-timers. The reason for this was a determination not to destroy the rural sector in the way the Enclosure Acts had destroyed it in Britain. While in Bavaria, I was told that in East Germany the farms had been amalgamated into collectives and there were no

independent farmers left. This was bad for society. The West German farmers certainly appeared content and for most of the last 20 years have enjoyed a very reasonable way of life in spite of the small size of their farms.

By a coincidence I revisited the same farm a few years later. We arrived with a Ministry official, and while we were having a cup of coffee a terrific argument broke out between the farmer and his son, who was now in charge, and the farmer's wife and daughter-in-law. It waxed fast and furious and at such a pace that I could not follow it with my rudimentary German. So I asked the officials about it as we drove away. They had saved some money, he told me. The women folk wanted it to buy a new stove and other home comforts and a car for themselves. But the son was going to spend it on five acres (2.02 hectares) of land which had come up for sale 3 km away and which was fragmented into six pieces. Why did he want to do that? I asked. Because, he said, his father had told him that in the terrible times of 1923 and 1947 when inflation had destroyed the economy, only those who had land could eat.

Farmers still have the same favoured place in the thinking of the German State, though there are murmurs from some of the Socialists that protection has gone too far. Their production certainly shows signs of becoming an embarrassment. More butter and beef go to Intervention buying than anywhere else and production from German soils is rather better than from a similar area of British land.

The French, on the other hand, have been much more ruthless in enlarging farms. Whole areas of the hill districts have been allowed to go out of production, and there has been a most generous policy of loans and grants to enable farmers to buy out their siblings. But this has a definite limit. The aim is a countryside of family farms, worked in general by the farmer and his wife. There is legislation against the formation of agricultural empires on the British model. It is impossible for anyone who is not a French farmer to buy a farm. Industrialists and institutions cannot buy, Even farmers who have bought farms cannot take them over unless they have secured the permission of an organisation called SAFER, which has a pre-emption on any land sale. You can buy a farm at auction, but the deal cannot go through unless SAFER allows it. This policy is in direct contradiction to the EEC rule that there should be no discrimination between nationalities or between fellow citizens. But as in so many things the French simply look after the French in a way the British never look after their own people in a Common Market context.

But don't get the idea that because of this cossetting French farmers are inefficient. Far from that. Grain output, for instance, has risen fourfold since 1950. France has some most wonderful land where cereal growing is the best in Europe. I used at one time to travel to Tours across the Beauce almost every year. At first all the work was being done by horses or even oxen. Sheep were kept in the buildings for dung. That was 30 years ago. I used to say to Ronie that it would make wonderful combine country and I would have liked to buy a farm. You could in those days, even as a foreigner. It would have been just perfect, with perhaps a little wine-growing farm 50 miles (80 km) south on the Loire. But I never had the money. Nowadays it is like the Middle West of the USA, with huge silos dominating the countryside, the fields a pattern of wheat and maize and not a head of stock to be seen anywhere. All these farms are either run by the farmer alone or perhaps with one man.

On this same trip I visited a farm in Eastern Normandy. Absolutely traditional with milking cows, beef cattle, pigs, hens and several different crops. The farmer and his six men were occupied on the 300 acres (121.4 hectares), and all had their meals in the farmhouse cooked by the farmer's wife. The fields were small and divided by hedges. Now the old man has retired. The eldest son has the farm, which he works himself. He grows sugar beet and wheat and fattens a thousand pigs a year. In addition he does the arable work on another 300 acres which belong to a sister and a neighbour, and they help him. His style of farming is absolutely first class. He has got rid of all the hedges, so the farm is just one field. But there is one snag. When his father dies the whole farm will have to be divided between the five remaining children. How much will he be able to keep? He already owns the house and one of his sisters has said she would leave him her share to farm. He might be able to buy a bit more with the help of a government loan, but he would probably end up with about half his present acreage.

Or take the case of another I met in the hills not far from Clermont Ferrand. He was a sheep farmer, at 3,000 ft (914 m), fattening lambs indoors most expensively. He had the whole of the family farm but his brother, who was a Chief of Police had agreed to let him have his share of the farm in exchange for a country villa. So my friend had had to build a monstrosity of a villa in the middle of the fields. There we met the policeman taking his ease, while his brother made hay. Fortunately his two sisters had become nuns and had renounced their worldly goods. If they had not, he told me, he would not have been able to farm at all. It was interesting to find that most farming families in the hill and mountain areas insisted on taking their share in cash, while in the better areas they were prepared to lease the land to the one who stayed at home. Rents are fixed by a complicated formula and security is almost complete.

Our visit to Italy was a bit of a shambles. We had been presented with a script to guide us by someone whose knowledge of Italy appeared to be limited in the first place. To begin with we were advised to go to Rome and ask Ashley Clarke for some addresses. When we got to Rome we found that a Sir Ashley Clarke had been the British Ambassador there but had left six months before. So we went to FAO, where we met one or two people who knew something of Italian farming and by degrees we fixed up a rough line of attack for the film I was engaged in making. Our original script kept saying things like 'slip over to the Po' or 'go to Piglio and watch the sheep leaving their stone huts to graze on the mountains at dawn, and watch them returning at dusk again'. Rome to the Po valley is some 400 miles – over mountain roads in those days. Piglio we never managed to find and you cannot film at dawn or dusk for obvious reasons.

Italian farming was very primitive in those days by our standards, with horses and oxen and a lot of hand labour. We were somewhat hampered by the fact that my producer, the late Ronald Webster, was obsessed with the idea of not spending money. In consequence we economised on interpreters. So when we found a whole troop of rather picturesquely dressed women reaping wheat with sickles by the roadside, we could not tell if they were in a film like *Bitter Rice,* a working party from a women's reformatory, or just the local WI doing a good turn!

We also came across princes and other noblemen in rather greater numbers than their importance merited. Or else we came across estates which had been taken over from some of the same gentry for closer settlement. One settlement near Rome was run by a battery of experts who obviously did not intend to allow the settlers, who had been landless labourers, to have a free hand. Nevertheless, the settlers seemed to be happy people receiving from the state an income and enough land on which to grow their own wine, according to notes I made at the time.

Near Assisi we called on a farm where the work was astonishingly primitive. Oxen were treading out the beans, and the livestock were on the ground floor of a very reasonable house. These conditions were repeated in all the hill and mountain areas. Here indeed were the problems which the CAP was designed to cure. Then we eventually got to the Po Valley and found a very different state of affairs, one to make one think. Here the farming was very commercialised. Huge apple orchards and vegetable farms cashing in on the early maturity due to the warm climate. This was good farming in every sense, helped by a most kindly government.

Later on this trip I was told by angry French and Dutch horticulturists that, thanks to transport subsidies, Italian produce could undercut theirs on the European markets. Italian farmers too received loans at very low interest rates – 1 to 3 per cent – over a very long term. That, for all the evidence of Italian inefficiency, the commercial farming was of a very high order. And this has endured to this day. Not long ago in the Po Valley I saw units for beef bulls bought as calves in Germany and France and fattened on maize silage and so on grown by co-operating farmers. The calves are some of the best produced. The buildings of these units are brand new and well designed, the management obviously first class. All the money for the buildings and the stock and the working capital had been provided at less than 3 per cent on 30-year loans. The most interesting thing to me about this very efficient enterprise was that this was a co-operative of Communist farmers.

By contrast, even 20 years ago the Dutch had a habit of rubbing in the efficiency of their systems. They were and are good and knew it to a degree of almost insufferable complacency. Because they had reclaimed much of their land from the waves they had an achievement to be proud of. Their markets were a model of co-operative discipline.

Everyone had spoken of the merits of the clock auction as a means of selling. Unlike in an ordinary auction, where the bids start low, the price is set high and the clock hand gradually drops until one of the buyers presses a switch which stops the hand and the deal is recorded. But what if no one presses the switch? The produce is then sent home to be destroyed. In other words the success of the Dutch system is the result of control of the market by a policy of buying in. The clock is no good without the minimum price. Something those who installed a Dutch type clock at a horticultural market in Cheltenham with a great fanfare of trumpets fail to take into account. The cost of buying in is pooled between all the vendors.

Some aspects of Dutch farming were again primitive by our standards. Some cows were being milked outside by hand, and produce was being shifted to market in punts and barges instead of lorries. Farms were very small but very well run. But one could already discern the pattern of future Dutch policy. Farming was an asset to be encouraged and exploited. It was no accident, but the result of positive encouragement, which enabled Holland to take advantage of the milk policy of the Common Market and produce four times the butter the country needed, so it could be exported or put into Intervention at Community expense.

Dutch policy makers saw their opportunity long before the EEC had

Harvesting beans for threshing, Italy.

Irrigating maize, Italy.

New silos on a Danish farm – real white elephants!

An old style Danish farmstead.

really got under way and prepared to take advantage of it. Although Dutch farmers were not treated particularly kindly by their governments, unlike the way French and German governments cherish theirs, Dutch governments saw to it that the opportunities were made to be exploited, particularly where advantage could be taken of EEC rules. The Dutch had also taken steps to avoid the high prices for cereal feeds that Common Market prices would mean. Long before the Community became really established they had organised the supply of manioc, orange peel and all sorts of cereal substitutes so that their livestock rations could be cheapened. Today Dutch feeds contain less than 20 per cent cereals as against more than 50 per cent in Britain.

The poor Danes had no such luck. They had a system of co-operative marketing which was second to none in providing what the consumer wanted, but a government which was never really interested in backing farmers to the hilt. The systems of farming were exactly what they had been in the thirties when I had spent some time there. The pig houses were the identical ones, highly labour intensive and their pigs were still of the same breeds. And they still are. But the Danes are an unhappy people now. They joined the EEC as we did in 1973 and, expecting a trebling of their prices, borrowed heavily to invest in almost everything. They have become very unstuck. About half the farmers in Denmark could be called insolvent, as it is doubtful if their assets would equal their liabilities. Hundreds are going bankrupt every year. Denmark is a very sad place.

What struck me most during that trip, and is still true today, was the dependence of European farming on the one-man family unit. Farms that employ labour are in even more of a minority than they were then and persist in Europe in only a few isolated areas. Instead of becoming uncompetitive with us because their scale is not as great as ours, they have become very effective indeed. For two reasons.

The first is political. It stands to reason that politicians of any country take more notice of numbers than of anything else. Farmers in Britain form about 2 per cent of the population. In Europe the proportion runs from about 8 per cent in France and Germany to 23 per cent in Ireland. Add to this the number of people with an indirect interest in land, such as family members letting their shares as in France, and the number reaches 20 per cent or more. Therefore all other member countries do tend to cherish their farmers and help them when they can, even if it is against the rules of the Community. Secondly, in the arena of low cost production a family farmer can undercut any farmer who has wages to pay. Something the devotees of big business here find hard to credit, but it is true.

11. The European Economic Community

There is no doubt at all that those who supported the founding of the European Economic Community were activated by the best of intentions. Their aim was so to integrate Europe that there could be no possible chance that the separate nations would ever again indulge in war. War in Europe would be a civil war, as it would if ever one should break out in the United States. In fact they were probably guided by the evolution of the United States which was only integrated through a civil war as horrible in its day as the last two European wars. By the 1950's Europe had been through its civil wars and the various countries had had enough.

What was so different between the end of the last war and that of earlier European wars which had devastated Europe and the world? I believe it was that for the first time in history both sides suffered almost equally. The winners certainly won, but only after devastation at home on an undreamt of scale exceeded only by the horrors the losers had to endure. Britain's losses were dreadful but bearable, those of occupied Europe and Russia indescribably worse, as were those of the villains, Germany and Italy, who started it all.

Now no one will be safe. The losing country could unleash an atomic bomb of such power that the winner would have nothing left to live for either. I sometimes think that the world reached a state of technical achievement similar to ours ages ago. Then some idiot let off an atomic device that started a chain reaction sufficient to destroy everything. From this, the planet has just evolved to its present state of technical achievement ready for a silly clot to destroy us all again. Everyone in the West, and the East for that matter, realises this, and is determined to prevent an atomic war at all costs. Because the great fear at the moment is of Russia, the countries outside the Soviet block just had to unite to protect themselves – as they have through NATO.

But the EEC is completely irrelevant to the defence issue. It is not a defensive pact but an attempt to integrate Europe in every sense into a homogeneous whole, regardless of national considerations. It is not directed towards an idealistic form of political union, but to forming a group of countries held together by links which have nothing to do with nationalism, patriotism or idealism. Its appeal has been couched in terms of self-interest. Every country's citizens were bribed by prospects of a better life through joining. In some mysterious way the sum of the members would be greater if they were united, than if they pursued their separate interests.

I have never believed it possible to impose from above, as the EEC is attempting to do today, an economic and political system which could suit countries from the Baltic to the Mediterranean, and from the Elbe to Western Ireland. The social, climatic and economic differences are far too great. Nor does the EEC recognise the enormous attraction that nationalism has for the bulk of the population. Man seems to need an identity. Just look at the way we in Britain take pride in our roots, particularly the Scots, the Welsh, the Irish and even the Cornish.

The real basis of the success of the USA was that its population was an amalgam of European nationalities which had lost their ethnic roots by emigrating. Even so Union was only achieved at the end of a Civil War which gave power to the centre. Many people have tried to unite the tribes of Europe by force, starting with the Romans and ending through Napoleon with Hitler. All have failed. Where I believe the EEC will fail is in its attempt to do the same thing, not by force, but by the implicit threat of being left outside the economic magic circle. This they have fostered through the attempted merging of the separate economies and the integration of the lives of all the peoples of Europe through the forced integration of more and more of their laws.

Few British people accepted that when we joined the Community, the laws and directives from Brussels would be superior to those of the British Parliament. Those who did point this out were treated as beneath contempt, as little Englanders who believed that nothing good would come from anyone across the Channel. Any deficiencies could soon be corrected through the democratic process, notably by the European Parliament. I would be the first to agree that Britain's Parliament is in no way superior to those operating in other member countries. Or that our law makers are any more disinterested or ethical than other European legislators. But the fact is that Westminster is *ours*, and is under our control. The European Parliament is, in my opinion, at present no more than a talking shop, where a collection of would-be politicians can enjoy themselves at our expense. It has no power as yet, except to sack the European Commission, a move which it is unlikely to take because its funds are provided through the Commission.

The Commission, made up of representatives of the member countries is charged with suggesting policies and then carrying out the decisions of the Council of Ministers. For instance, the Agricultural Price Review is first worked out by the Commission and presented to Ministers. The Agricultural Ministers can accept it or, if they wish, alter it. The Commission takes it back and tries to make it fit the demands of the separate interests. This may or may not be accepted. If it isn't, it is again sent back and again returned. This game of political ping-pong can go on as long as the endurance of the Ministers lasts. Eventually a compromise is reached which has more to do with expediency than with good judgement. No one is really satisfied.

Over the years I have attended a number of these Council meetings in Brussels as a journalist. They are all of a pattern – at least those dealing with agriculture are. The venue is the Charlemagne building, a high rise complex next door to the Berlaymont where the main offices are. I have never been to the Council room on the top floor, but have remained with the Press in the lounge downstairs.

This has one redeeming feature – a bar where sandwiches and drinks are served at very low prices while the Ministers are sitting. As soon as the Council goes into recess the bar is firmly closed and any drinks have to be bought at the very high priced Belgian cafés outside. Or one has to go to the Press room in the main building where the drinks, when it is open, are again very reasonably priced. The Press lounge also has a typewriter room where last time I was there all the English language typewriters were out of order – sabotaged, it was hinted, by the French – and the usual telex and telephone facilities. The Council expects news to be made and spread throughout the world.

Ministers are supposed to be in secret session, but as with Mrs Thatcher's Cabinet and probably every other cabinet in the world, the sessions are leaked assiduously and purposely by all the participating Ministers. The whole effect on the Press room is of conducting a battle blindfolded in a fog with only word of mouth to convey intelligence. A very biased word of mouth it is too. This is because as soon as the session has started the separate Ministers begin to send down messages to their acolytes from their own national Press waiting below. Every now and then the national spokesman comes down and gives his fellows a blow-by-blow account of what is happening upstairs. The spokesman is closely surrounded by his countrymen and those not understanding the language are left in some confusion.

But such is the fellowship of the international Press that they will share each other's secrets – for, of course, they are not secrets. Most of this goes on through the late afternoon and well into the night. Various deadlines have to be met in national capitals. *The Financial Times* has three so-called deadlines, about 7.30 and 10.30 pm and 3.30 am, coinciding with the three editions. The first edition is the most important, so the journalist is under great pressure to file a good story by then with an accurate forecast of what will happen. That is if it has not yet been decided. Everyone else is in the same boat, so there is frenzied activity as thousands and thousands of words are shouted down telephones or incessantly telexed. In such circumstances it is not possible to make considered judgements, or even be sure, what the German spokesman said, for instance, to say nothing of the Danish or the Greek. Sometimes the Press room is invaded by groups of farmers' representatives who barrack Ministers and others who appear from time to time.

It is important to realise here that the Council of Ministers is the final authority. The Commission has no power to overrule any of its judgements. This was particularly borne out in a very bad tempered meeting in 1974 when the beef industry was in a good deal of trouble. To put things right the Council proposed as one of the measures to ban some imports of beef from third countries, either directly or by punitive levies.

The President of the Commission heard of this and instructed a British Commissioner, Christopher Soames, now Lord Soames, to try and prevent it. Soames was unwell at the time and sent his assistant down to convey the message but, for all the good it did, the time was wasted. The Council was determined to do something for beef farmers and in the event the only thing they could do was reduce pressure on the market. The British Minister of Agriculture at the time, Fred Peart, started off by opposing the move, but then in the interest of being 'Communautaire' accepted a package which included the ban, so it came into being. He thoroughly upset the Australians and others who were trying to maintain a presence in the British market.

It should be remembered that the Council of Ministers has to have unanimity. There is no majority decision making. For this we have to thank General de Gaulle who forced this rule through as a price for France remaining within the Community. This is a point of view I agree with entirely. I don't believe the States of Europe are ready for the absolute democratic process yet. Anyway it would be fatal for any politician on the European scene to disregard the wishes of the folks back home. After all, they are the people who send him to the Ministry and ultimately to Europe.

This is the background to the unedifying late night quarrels which go on at every meeting. Every Minister is fighting for a particular interest which is far more important in the minds of his constituents than abstract theories of European unity. Nor are they particularly aware of all the issues on which the Commission itself gives its considered (or unconsidered) opinion.

I remember on one occasion the milk surplus was causing considerable concern. Indeed it always does. There was a theory that one way to reduce it would be to encourage the pig keepers of Europe to use skimmed milk powder rather than soya bean meal to feed their stock. So almost at the end of a Council meeting, and before the British contingent realised what had happened, a temporary levy was put on imports of soya.

I learnt sometime afterwards that this suggestion came from a Commission official who, when asked at the eleventh hour what could be done about the skimmed milk surplus, suggested as a casual aside that a tax on soya would help. So it came in and cost me as a farmer, among others, quite a lot of money. Skimmed milk powder has only about half the protein of soya meal and there was no way we could use it without great added expense on the pig rations. In the end the levy had to be removed under pressure from the users and from the USA, the major source of supplies.

But we haven't heard the end of the attacks on soya for a long time yet, on two counts. The increase in the costs of disposing of the butter surplus and its gradual replacement by margarine is bringing a demand from some countries for a tax on edible oils, among which of course is soya oil. This is reinforced by the belief that much of the excess milk production in Europe is caused by feeding soya meal, the residue after the extraction of the oil, along with other feeds to produce milk instead of using just home grown grass and forage crops. There is quite a lot of truth in this, but soya is also fed to pigs and poultry, so any tax on its import would also affect pig and poultry farmers quite seriously.

This is well known, of course, and is also known to the Ministers and their advisers. But we see the Ministers from countries where most milk comes from forage – Ireland, Germany and France – banging the table and demanding the restriction of soya imports regardless of the harm it does to other facets of livestock farming. The only logical answer to the surplus crisis would be to make those countries producing too much suffer the consequences in some way. This already works with sugar beet. Production is regulated by quotas operated right down to the farm gate. This means that a farmer knows that if he plants an excess acreage he will be made to suffer through having to sell his surplus at a very low price.

At one time the British Government favoured this approach and it is believed to have had some support from the Germans – the Farmers' Union there in particular. But it was attacked by the Commission and the other Ministers. The Commission attacked it because it destroyed the concept of a Common Market in which competition determined the ultimate price and would brook no artificial interference with it. This of course is complete hypocrisy or perhaps a wilful obstinacy to face facts. No Government will allow its producers to suffer too much and every Government makes some provision to help its lame ducks. The means used may be illegal under Community rules and could even cause the offending state to be hauled up before the European Court.

This is what happened in the lamb war of the late '70s. At the time the French, by a particularly non-Communautaire interpretation of the rules of free trading, were preventing the import of British lamb. They were twice brought before the European Court, were found guilty and ordered to open their frontiers, but they did nothing about it. At that time I took part in a French television programme with M. Mehaignerie, the French Minister of Agriculture. 'What,' I asked him, 'do you think of the judgements against you?' 'It's true', he replied, 'that I have suffered two adverse judgements. But I am still in good health and I am unlikely to go to prison'. And he persisted in his refusal to accept imports until the implementation of a new regulation on sheep meat which made the export of British lamb to France almost impossible.

There is a good deal of talk about reforming the Common Agricultural Policy. But because eight of the ten countries like it as it is – and if Spain and Portugal join it will be ten out of 12 – very little will be done as long as the two paymasters, Britain and Germany, go on signing the cheques. The United States is often given as an example of a country which evolved a form of agricultural unity by common prices within a large country with many variations of soil and climate.

This is abundantly true. But the evolution of American farming into the most favourable zones has brought a profound change in the social and economic set-up of the whole country. Originally US farming was confined to the Eastern seaboard. Now it has largely moved to the Middle

West and the irrigated deserts of the South-West and California. I was having a few days holiday in New Hampshire once and, leaving a picnic site to stroll through the woods, I came across stone walls and farm buildings such as can be found in the Cotswolds today. The whole of the farming in that area had succumbed to economic pressures, and the farmers had just moved away. The land was steep, stony and difficult. Few Americans will farm such country, or can afford to.

If you transpose that sort of situation to Europe, many parts of Britain would not qualify to compete with better favoured areas like Central France, Germany or the Low Countries. In a real EEC with common prices and conditions, we would be in deep trouble. It is because I don't want to see the greater part of Britain reverting to scrub and recreation areas, that I am opposed to a continuation of the Common Agricultural Policy to its logical conclusion. I don't quarrel with other countries who look after their own farmers, despite the rules. We should imitate, not decry them.

It has often been said that the CAP has made the food supplies of the member countries safe against world supply and price fluctuations. This is nonsense. In the eight years of our membership from 1973 to 1981, world prices for the main commodities have been consistently below the EEC level by a substantial amount. With two exceptions – for grain a brief period in 1974, and for sugar during 1974–75 and for a few months in 1980.

Because of the natural shortage of available farming land Britain has still to import between 30 and 35 per cent of temperate foods. These have all been imported at world prices plus a levy to bring them up to EEC levels or from the Continent at the existing high prices. It is nonsense to claim, as the apologists of the Community reiterate, that world prices are a figment of a little Englander's imagination. They exist for everything, and with those exceptions have always been below EEC ones by 20 to 50 per cent.

It must also be remembered that the CAP has had a deplorable effect on the economies of other farming countries. This is because of the policy of exporting surpluses with subsidies designed to match the competition in any country in the world. It is ironical that the main beneficiaries of these subsidies are the Russians and other Communist countries, who don't seem to be able to grow enough food for themselves. The money raised from the taxpayer and consumer to finance this policy could, with profit I believe, be used to better advantage. The Communists must think we are mugs.

In the Referendum on the EEC I voted 'No', and in fact drove 300 miles to register my vote. Would I do so again if, as seems likely, the question could be put to the test? This puts me in a bit of a dilemma. I am an old man and at 70 plus do not feel I should take part in a decision which would affect the lives of many who would be much more dependent on the results than myself. But this I would say. There is a perfectly logical case for remaining outside on the grounds of sovereignty. Sovereignty is considered pretty old hat these days, but it really means that a country should be able to do what it thinks is best for its own people. The gradual imposition of rules from an unrepresentative Commission in Brussels and from Councils of Ministers and European Parliaments where we would not have a veto, would be very dangerous.

I believe we should go back to first principles and stick to NATO, several of whose members are not in the EEC, and have a go at restructuring the European Free Trade Area in a loose organisation. From this more unity could well grow. Forcible integration into Europe under the present arrangements is almost bound to fail.

12. 'Yes Minister'. A Bed of Nails

There is a story that when, in 1940, Winston Churchill called the late Lord Hudson, at that time a Tory Minister, to say that he was to be Minister of Agriculture, Hudson said, on putting down the phone, 'Some enemy has done this to me.' In point of fact, Lord Hudson acquitted himself well as Minister. But then he was backed by the resources of a government determined to extract the utmost food from Britain's farms. He had not only the Cabinet but the Law and public opinion on his side. What Hudson meant, I believe, was that no ambitious politician had ever risen far after being Minister of Agriculture. Certainly not to Prime Minister. But Heathcote Amory, later Lord Amory, became Chancellor of the Exchequer. Why farming should inflict this blight on its Ministers, I don't know. I can only conjecture that it was always a minor Ministry before the War, when we were in the throes of the cheap food policy. Once food scarcities were no longer a problem it became a backwater again.

It is true that the Ministry has become more important in the public eye since we joined the EEC. Ministers meet monthly in Brussels to dispute the various things that are disputed about, and have a sort of spurious importance because they are always in the news. But don't be misled by that. British Ministers of Agriculture are now in the last resort dependent on decisions in Brussels, not No. 10 Downing Street. Farmers here don't seem to have got that message yet, and still badger the Minister as if the EEC did not exist. Ministers of Agriculture have another cross to bear – the basic ingratitude of farmers to those set over them. They are never satisfied, and probably never will be, however much a Minister strains himself to look after their interests. But there was one notable exception to this.

The late Tom Williams, a miner's MP from Yorkshire, served in the Ministry as Parliamentary Secretary under Hudson during the War, then as Minister from 1945 to 1951. As far as I could gather, he knew very little about farming. But he knew how to make friends with farmers, starting with the post-war President of the NFU, James Turner, later Lord Netherthorpe. He certainly served his Government very well. During the whole of his period in office food was short and in a free market farmers could have obtained very high prices for all they produced. Instead, he instituted the Agriculture Act, 1947, which set out in highly qualified terms that farmers would be guaranteed prices sufficient to sustain the production of 'that part of the nation's food it was essential to grow in this country'. The measure of his success as a Minister was that farmers took this as a form of price support, when in truth it was simple price control. After the Labour Government went out of office in 1951, food surpluses began to appear and the wartime controls were wound down. But all the strife was between his successors and farmers who had to face price stagnation and actual reduction, particularly in cereal prices. Small wonder then that Tom Williams is still regarded as the patron saint of the NFU.

I did not meet Williams until after he had left office, but I then found him a decent modest man, very proud of his origins. He was the son of a miner who had become a Union official, even though he could neither read nor write. Williams told me he used to attend his father's Union meetings as a schoolboy, so that he could keep the books. His delivery of a speech in a flat Yorkshire accent was dull in the extreme, but he had a way of defusing an angry farmers' meeting by projecting himself as a reasonable man it would be positively unkind to attack. With this manner he could gain support for the most outrageous propositions.

I once attended a special NFU meeting in London called to protest against one of the price review determinations of the time. Farmers all over the country were up in arms, and there was a threat that the complex systems of control of marketing could suffer, or that production could fall. As always, farmers were asking for full recoupment of recent cost increases. Turner as President was having a hard job keeping the Union in order. In the end, Tom Williams himself arrived to talk us round. We were asked to stand as he came in, as a mark of respect, and did so rather grudgingly. Then he stood up in his wing collar and talked us into submission. He understood the farmers' fears, he said. He would undertake to see that their incomes did not fall below those of other rural people. The country was in grave straits and depended on the good citizenship of its farmers as it did on that of every section of the community.

When he finished he was cheered to the echo as he walked out. When the meeting resumed, Turner put it to us that his proposition should be accepted. But what, I asked the President, had the Minister really meant? Who were the rural dwellers with whom we were to be compared? The formula, I was told, had not yet been agreed. Could we have an idea then whom the President and the Minister had had in mind when they reached their agreement? Rural dwellers were not so plentiful that he could have had no no idea. In the end the reply came that it would of course include the village shopkeeper and postman, among others. Was he, then, in favour of reducing farmers' incomes to that of the postman? But this time the meeting was thoroughly impatient with me. The President made an appeal to our statesmanship and we went home. From then on, although I was quite active in the NFU and was a Council member for a while, I never felt inhibited in attacking the leadership from within the organisation. I always thought Jim Turner was completely under the spell of Tom Williams' most reasonable approach. He felt it his duty to co-operate with him as far as he could, and he did with other Ministers as well. As an honest and patriotic man he saw virtue in co-operating with the Government of the day as an alternative to aggression and confrontation.

Some Governments did not always have the same need to charm the farmers on to their side, particularly in the pre-war days. One exception was Neville Chamberlain, who plucked the late Sir Reginald Dorman Smith from the Presidency of the NFU and put him into the Cabinet as Minister of Agriculture. I can remember little about this tenure, but it kept farmers quiet until the War came along and they were needed. He started the expansion programme within the limits set by the Treasury. When the Coalition Government was formed, however, Hudson took on and Dorman Smith became Governor of Burma. I always thought him unlucky not to have had the wartime job.

Williams was succeeded by Sir Thomas Dugdale, who became the first Lord Crathorne. He was, I firmly believe, the last gentleman in British politics. A very nice knight of the shires. His undoing came through no fault of his at all, unless obedience to a principle is a fault. He inherited what was called the Crichel Down case. Crichel Down was an area in East Dorset taken over by the RAF before the War as a bombing range. The family who owned it received compensation which was considered reasonable at the time of the take over. After the War the RAF gave up the land, and the local War Agricultural Committee took over farming it and eventually agreed to let it to a local farmer.

Meanwhile the family of the previous owners ran a long campaign to try and get the land back, on the principle that once the Government no longer needed it for their purposes, it should revert to them. The Labour Government, which always leaned a little towards State control, did nothing about it until, after much argument, a Commission of Enquiry was set up which decided that the land should be handed back, in spite of the refusals of previous Ministers to agree to this. Dugdale had to announce the Government's agreement to this in the House. He did so, then promptly resigned, although he had had nothing to do with the case at all. He maintained that he was bound by the convention of Ministerial responsibility, although the whole affair was a classic of bureaucratic bungling. Would that there were more like him.

The next Minister to make any real impact was Christopher Soames. It was his task to end the system of open-ended guarantees which had sustained farming for many years, and replace it with production which fitted the Government's idea of the market. He did not make too good an impression at the start. First of all, he was Churchill's son-in-law and he was given to rather Churchillian poses and expressions and at first little else. Beneath that facade though, there was a very able man carrying out a most unpopular policy, that of limiting the extent of the guarantees. He could be very rough indeed, both with farmers and with his own Civil servants. He knew nothing of the subject when appointed, and made some notable gaffes in interviews, but he was a very quick learner. In the end he commanded the respect, if not the affection, of farmers.

This policy restricted farmers' incomes throughout the sixties even more effectively, I thought, than Tom Williams had done earlier. But while Williams did it by political skills, Soames used a sort of arrogant indifference which used to exasperate farmers' leaders and to some extent the Press. After interviewing him on a number of occasions, I found him intellectually the peer of most of his fellow politicians. But his manner was so much against him that after losing his seat in 1964 he never found another. Harold Wilson made him Ambassador to Paris, a crafty move to get him out of politics for a while, and Heath made him a Commissioner in Brussels. I saw him at the Commission several times, when he was not only ill, but frustrated in the extreme by the antics, the often irresponsible antics, of the Council of Ministers, particularly in relation to the Common Agricultural Policy.

Fred Peart, who succeeded him, had to carry on some of his policies and faced some very angry audiences for a while. He had been Tom Williams' Parliamentary Secretary and pursued his mentor's approach to farmers as far as he could. This was particularly obvious when he reappeared at the Ministry in 1974. From then on he and the then President of the NFU, Sir Henry Plumb, recreated the Turner/Williams partnership. I thought that by this time Peart had become almost excessively pro-Market, making up for his past opposition, no doubt. I used to attend some of the Councils in Brussels and it did seem to me he agreed on certain issues simply because of his determination to be Communautaire and not rock the boat.

He was quite a gambler and would offer the most complicated odds on almost any subject. I remember he once tried to get me to bet on Newcastle United winning both the Cup and the League. I demurred. Then he asked if there was a local football club in my area. Southampton was the only one I could think of. 'I will lay you a hundred to one against Southampton winning the FA Cup', he offered. 'Will you put £1 on?' We were in the bar of the Europa Hotel in Brussels and I said I would sooner buy him a drink and I did. Of course, Southampton went on to win the Cup that year! He was bitterly disappointed in being moved up into the Lords just before he could claim to be the longest serving Minister of Agriculture and also before he could chair the Ministerial Council in Brussels. But his basic inability to be really nasty to the NFU and the Council of Ministers led to his replacement by John Silkin, on the whole a most competent operator.

Silkin's brief was to stop further devaluations of the Green Pound and to stop any increase in Community spending if he could. The Green Pound was the exchange rate between the European unit of account, in which all Community farm prices were fixed, and sterling. Because of currency instability this was very variable and some of the time the Green Pound gap, as it was called, was some 40 per cent. This led to what were called Monetary Compensatory Amounts or MCA's, which acted as a subsidy on EEC imports and a levy on our exports to the others. They certainly kept prices down and frustrated farmers but they were a part of the effort to keep down the cost of living. Silkin started with the advantage that he did not like the Community, had voted against joining, and would be quite prepared to come out of it again. He wasn't impressed by the NFU's call for complete devaluation of the Green Pound and the end of the MCA's. He became even more disliked by farmers than Soames had been, probably because he was a Labour man. In Brussels he was quite popular among other Ministers who in their pursuit of national interests could be very rough indeed. They were, and are, all Silkins.

I have had the opportunity to watch the behaviour of many

Agricultural Ministers here and in Europe and there does seem to be an essential difference between the two. European Ministers represent their farmer constituents in a way no British Ministers have ever done in my experience. British Governments lay down policy and Ministers have to follow it or lose their jobs, vide the replacement of Fred Peart. European Ministers always seem to be looking after their farmers regardless of the rest of the policy being followed by their governments, most of which are biased towards their farmers anyway. They have never yet had a cheap food policy. I am sure this is due to the basic structure of their societies. Farmers are a declining force in most European countries now, but even at 10 per cent, the present average, represent four times the British proportion.

But that is not all. Thanks to the operation of the Code Napoléon, which lays down that property must be equally divided between the members of a deceased person's family, land ownership in Europe is infinitely fragmented. In some countries and districts of countries, though not in all, this has led to the most absurd layout of farms and estates. In general, the practice is for one of the family to take on the farm and either buy out the rest or, as often happens in France, to rent the others' shares from them. I was on a 400 acre rented farm in France once where the tenant told me he had 30 landlords, none of whom he had ever seen. These fragmented parcels of land had been bought and sold over the years. Rents were fixed by a tribunal and as far as I can see everyone seemed to be happy. But the political weight of all those interested in the prosperity in land through the rents received is very much stronger than that of the individuals actually farming it. Instead of 10 per cent being actively interested in farming, the figure in much of Europe must be two or three times that. All with a cash or family interest in the perpetuation of prosperous farming.

Land reform: a smallholder's steading in Columbia.

PART 5: LATIN AMERICA

13. Columbia. Are Co-operatives the Answer?

The South American Handbook, an absolute necessity for anyone travelling in Latin America, warns that the inhabitants of Bogotá, the capital of Colombia, are a thievish lot. Put your hand out of a car to indicate a turn and in no time at all someone will have snicked off your wrist watch. Pickpockets abound, and even public transport is not safe. Buses are hi-jacked in motion! With this sort of warning, we emptied our pockets of most valuables, avoided crowds where we could, and hired taxis for the longer journeys. We were taken for a ride nevertheless. Julio was waiting outside the hotel on our first morning and claimed that he knew how to look after foreigners. I was spending the day visiting offices, trying to get help to research on land reform.

Warned by the SAH, I demanded a quotation for the daily hire. It was very reasonable indeed. So much so that when I paid him at the end of the day I felt I was underpaying him, particularly as he told me he was assisting two of his children to go through college. My soft heart was a mistake. For the rest of the week I was there he somehow or other managed to increase the proportionate charge, until on the final trip to the airport he stung me for the balance of my Colombian currency. It was all done so quietly and with a sort of humility that, hardened as I am, I could scarce forbear a tear as we shook hands and he wished me a safe return. But I suppose it was better than being robbed in the flesh or mugged or taken to bits by one of the con artists, who are supposed to be the next step up in Colombian crime.

I had secured a number of introductions from the Embassy in London, the Coffee Board and others, so my path would be smoothed. But I found that here, as in most other places I have visited, the locals have plenty more to do than worry about visiting journalists. What it amounted to was to find the address of the relevant office, walk in and try and impress the receptionist with the importance of my paper. This is a tricky one. I don't carry a *Financial Times* card, for the simple reason that outside England, and sometimes even within it, the *FT* is thought to be the business section of *The Times* of London. So during my spiel I announce that I come from *The Times*. This opens many doors which would otherwise remain shut. Everyone has heard of *The Times* of London, so one is half-way in.

Once with a senior man, I try and speak to him in English. If he can't, I have to revert to Spanish, which I can fortunately understand. I explain that the readers of my paper are desperate for news of the progress of land reform in Colombia, or wherever I happen to be. This immediately leads to the production of a man in charge of the project. In almost all cases the first concrete reaction is a shower of paper, of statistics. I have drawers full of them still from every country in the world. This is fine, I say, and invaluable as background, but what I really need is to see some of this work on the ground. I explain that in some other countries I have visited I have found the statistics are seldom borne out by reality. When could I venture to some of the sites?

This causes a minor consternation. Give me the addresses, I'd say. Julio is waiting outside and he would be only too pleased to take me there. With my knowledge of Spanish I should be able to get all the information I need. This would not do at all. But as it happens – a common phrase in these negotiations – a high-level deputation is going down to the Magdalena River area tomorrow and we should be very pleased for you and your wife to accompany them. This technique has never failed and I have seen much of the world through it.

Bogotá is about 8,000 ft above sea level and the climate and the farming is very European in style with temperate crops and cattle. The farms are large and economic and there is little suggestion of land reform here. The owners are too important politically. But within a couple of hours' drive it is possible to drop right down to the tropics. I made two trips to the lowlands. The first, to investigate land reform, was accompanied by a young woman with a very good command of English and a profound hatred of the CIA, which she had picked up while at university in the United States. Her interest in land reform was minimal, I thought, except to achieve some political advantage in future elections. Her idea of land reform was to remove the rich, who had plenty of cash salted away in the States or Europe anyway, and give the land to the peasants, who would then become free men.

Her companion was a most earnest young man who was determined to break up the big estates, many of which he claimed were under-farmed. But this had to be done in an orderly manner and the peasants so liberated had to be drafted into co operatives so they would gain the advantages of scale. His was the idealistic approach, and the first settlement we visited had been organised on these lines and was obviously a showplace. We met settlers living in rather pleasant surroundings amid the gardens and banana trees. All production was sold through the central office which provided finance and good advice.

We then went to a further estate which had just been taken over, and attended a meeting of the one-time workers who had been given the land. The meeting was held in the old landowner's house. After a searing attack on the previous owner, the settlers were given a lecture on the benefits of co-operation. The applause then turned to shouts of anger and the young co-operator began to get flustered. 'What do you want, then?' he cried. 'Here is the Government doing all it can, and now you have your freedom and your land. Why don't you co-operate?'

Hereupon a rather wild-looking fellow with what I took to be a pistol in his trouserband replied in these terms. 'I am a Colombian Campesino. For centuries we have fought, first against the Spaniards and then the rich. We have been slaves too long to wish to exchange the slavery of a rich old woman, the previous owner, for a co-operative run by the Government. All we need is a hectare each to call our own, and our liberty.' Everyone cheered, and the platform retreated in some confusion.

This in a nutshell has been the problem of land reform in most of the developing countries. Certainly in all I have visited. Co-operation may be the ideal answer in a perfect world, but co-operatives can become just as unpopular as previous exploitation. This is bound to be so. Bureaucratic mistakes are inevitably made, and the point of being a free man insufficiently appreciated. Even the progressive British farmers don't co-operate very well. Why on earth should uneducated peasants? In Colombia independence has some substance. In the low country climate, I was assured, a man could keep quite a large family on a hectare, and housing and clothing needs are few. There would be plenty of time to idle, go to fairs or get drunk.

Our guides were really shocked that I had witnessed their confusion, but I told them that independence was really man's most earnest craving – often more than sex. Our lady companion was shocked. Such desires should be subordinated to the good of all. There could be no progress without an orderly approach to the business of living. Dialectical materialism pointed the way. I did not know which way it pointed, but in the course of many investigations of Latin American land reform, I found the only ones which were really working were in Peru, where the then military government refused to take any but the most destitute members of society into a co-operative. Anyone who had been independent before was forbidden to join because they had learnt the bad habits of drink and going to market. This is obviously the way to make co-operation work unless the co-operators are the sophisticated Danes or other Europeans.

I remember visiting a village in the Ivory Coast and talking to the headman. He asked me what the prices of cocoa and coffee were on the world market. 'Ah', he said, 'we only get a quarter of that'. 'How come?' I asked. 'Well', he said, 'you have visited the Cocoa and Coffee headquarters in Abidjan, the capital. That is where the money goes.' The Colombians have a celebrated Coffee Board, which I visited. Through this all the coffee in the country is channelled for marketing. Great play is made of the fact that its members include the smallest of the growers with a production of only a few bags, a mule load in fact. The small growers actually dominate the membership but in terms of produce sold the larger growers have by far the greatest influence, though they are much fewer in number. Who is to say that the decisions of the Board are in the best interests of all, and not those of the few big boys?

In Colombia, though, I did not see the absolute squalor and poverty of the Peruvian Indians, for instance. There is a drift from the villages to the towns, mainly Bogotá, but because there is plenty of land and a fairly benign tropical climate, life is bearable as compared with that in many other countries. Some of this may be due to the character of the people themselves, who have a history of armed revolt. There were several bodies of revolutionaries operating in the outlying districts at the time of my visit. The Government itself changes hands regularly between the two main parties after a long revolution in the 40's and 50's in which thousands died. By all accounts the main source of the peasants' income now is the cultivation of marijuana and other drugs for the American market, something about which the central government can do little.

My friend Antonio – he is still my friend, though we have not seen each other for years – rang me at my hotel. 'Mr John', he said, (he spoke English very well) 'I have been told you like cattle'. 'I do indeed', I replied. 'Well, come and see me. My office is just round the corner.' His office was in a modern building, and the ante-room was full of obvious country people waiting patiently. The receptionist showed me straight in to where Antonio, young and very nicely dressed, was confronted by a weeping woman. She refused to be comforted by his soft phrases, so he called his receptionist to ease her out. As a parting shot she turned to him and said, 'For the sake of myself, my seven children, my old parents and my dead husband, who was your friend, see that justice is done.'

'A difficult job, mine', said Antonio, when the door was shut. 'I am in charge of the cattle ranches along the Magdalena River and her husband was killed a week or two ago by a gang of bandits who drove off the cattle. Now the family and the ranch are in my trust.' He was, I gathered, a sort of public trustee and controlled a lot of cattle belonging to the unfortunates, of which there were many in the country. He also ran a large cattle auction in the low country. This, he told me, was a political appointment, a sop for having come too low on the list of candidates to qualify for a seat in government. But still he had hopes of getting in at the next elections – the only way for a poor man to succeed in Colombia.

'Come with me and see my cattle tomorrow. I will call for you at 7 am in a cross-country vehicle with plenty of room for you and your wife.' At seven we were ready and waited with growing impatience until 9.30. I had almost given him up when he arrived in a short wheel based Land Rover, accompanied by his wife, three boys, a dog and a saturnine individual whom he introduced as a political aide. The ladies took the front seat and I joined the rest in the back. The boys quarrelled and the dog growled all the way, while I crouched in my seat and developed dreadful cramp. The political aide wrapped himself in a shawl and said nothing. We passed the stages from the temperate highlands to the tropic fairly fast, and turned off for the banks of the Magdalena, a fast stream of rather muddy water.

It was very hot and humid, and I envied the fishermen I could see standing up to their waists in the water casting their nets. We drew up at a restaurant, no more than a palm-thatched shelter with tables, and ordered fish for lunch. We should be back in about three hours, we said. As we left I saw an elderly man who had been sitting at one of the tables go outside, pick up a net and walk towards the river. In that hot climate the fish *had* to be fresh.

We continued on to the sale yards. These are, of course, the same all the world over but the Colombian cattlemen are a special breed. Dressed in shirt and trousers and a trilby hat, every man carried a towel. This was variously used to swat flies, wipe the sweat off their faces, encourage the horse, push on the cattle or just worn round the neck. Everyone had one and all were of the same rough textured pattern. One or two had pistols at their belts, but the rest were unarmed.

The main talk was of the poor price they were getting for their cattle, as the Peruvian market, one of the main outlets, was in some sort of trouble. The other plague were the revolutionaries who had been killing the odd beast for food. They hoped Antonio could induce the authorities to take some action over this. The cattle were the humped white Brahmin type common in the tropics and looked in reasonable order. They could thrive, they told us, on the natural pasture that grew after the trees and scrub had been cleared.

We returned for lunch, and found the table spread with banana leaves on each of which the proprietor dumped a large fish, rather like bass, and some vegetables, including some very tough plantains or bananas cut green. There were no knives or forks. Picking the fish to pieces is difficult but possible when one is hungry. As we were finishing, sundry small boys appeared, and Antonio told me they would take the scraps. I could not finish my fish because my particular attendant watched every piece into my mouth with increasing dismay. I had to hand over a lot.

We then went to visit a leading rancher who lived on what seemed to be the only raised piece of ground on a vast plain. There was mud and water everywhere and the mosquitoes rose in clouds. The house looked a barrack but once inside we were in another world. Some air conditioning, polished floors, and bookcases stuffed with the best of Western literature in several languages. How long the owners spent on the ranch I have no idea. The family had been educated in the States and Europe. It could be that the pressure for land reform was keeping them at home. There were several cases of farms being taken, even when the owners had been away for only a few days.

The contrast between this luxurious living and the shacks in which many of the workers lived was extreme. Even the better housing we were shown consisted of little more than concrete barracks with a minimum of comfort. However the working class people had an independent look and the differences appeared to be more of wealth than class.

Antonio was a good democratic politician, so the next day, after a very hot night temperature-wise in a very basic guest house, he decided to fulfil a political chore. It was probably the object of the whole expedition. 'It is only a few minutes off the road home', he said, as he turned off the main asphalt on to an earth track. There had been a good deal of rain and the Land Rover skidded alarmingly, but we kept to the road. Before long we came on another Land Rover on its side in the ditch, surrounded by a crowd of the locals.

Ever a man of action, Antonio produced a rope and with us all pushing and our vehicle pulling we got it out and on its wheels. It turned out that this was the village bus. When they were ready to start, after suitable speeches of thanks, 23 people got into one short wheel base Land Rover! As we drove on, Antonio said that he was nursing this constituency and the purpose of the detour was to hand over some money to the village to repair this road, and also to build a new bridge over a fairly fast-flowing river. His party had extracted the money from the Government, and now he was going to get what credit he could from being the messenger.

The village was a collection of unpainted corrugated iron shacks and sheds with a railway running the length of it and a cross-roads leading to the bridge to be repaired, a suspension affair only suitable for people on foot and horses. The mountain rose straight up from the far side of the river and there were only tracks on the other side. Every now and then a train of pack mules came down the mountain, crossed the bridge, and were led into one or other of the open sheds along the road. These were coffee warehouses and this was the harvest from farms and villages many hours' journey into the mountains.

It was a Sunday, but business still seemed to be as usual. Some stores were open and there was a butcher's shop with some very revolting wares. After the ceremony of handing over the cheque, for which I was made official photographer, we adjourned to the pub, a long verandah where benches and tables had been set out. Beer was served and speeches made. The Colombian barmaid has got just the right idea. As soon as the top is off one bottle, she puts another down, and never stops as far as I could see. Every now and then one of the leading local politicians would present us with a bottle of spirit, a sort of gin, in case the beer was too weak. There was also a jukebox being worked by the children, but this was soon sabotaged by the politicians who wanted to hear themselves speak. Every few minutes a train came puffing into the village with crowds of people hanging on to the outside of the carriages, even on the engine. Some of them got off and joined us, others jumped on. Tickets were unnecessary for the Campesinos, I was told. After all, they were only exercising their democratic rights.

As the morning drew on the speeches grew more impassioned. Suddenly I was called upon to bring a message from across the water. My Spanish was by that time fluent if somewhat inexact. I toasted our two countries and expressed the fervent hope that Antonio would be elected next time. Loud cheers greeted this remark and I went on to praise his wife, who would be a stalwart help to her husband in his quest for the post of President. I am not sure if my phrasing was accurate for at this point she blushed and squeezed my hand and he said firmly. 'Basta!' – 'Enough!'

Then someone at the end of the building said something about eating. By this time it was midday. Someone else said *gallina,* chicken. Sure enough there was a squawking, a cloud of feathers drifted round the corner, and a fire was kindled. We went on drinking and talking. I interviewed everyone from the Chief of Police to the two winners of the local beauty contest and included a character who maintained a wife and 12 children on less than half a hectare. His children were a worry to him. There was a school in the village but all they could think about was how to get to university in Bogotá. They took no interest in the farm. Did I have the same trouble at home? Yes, I said. It was all the fault of education. Thereupon he embraced me and bought me a beer. Suddenly there was a series of explosions. 'La Revolucion?' I asked. No, simply a juego a game. We went to have a look. It was a sort of French boules but with metal balls containing percussion caps. When they touched another ball these went off. It saves a lot of argument, I was told.

During a break in the proceedings I sauntered off into the railway siding to answer a call of nature. I thought I was being followed but was eventually surprised by the twin beauty queens. Their intentions, alas, were entirely honourable. Would I take their photos? When we got back to the pub together we were greeted by wild cheering and the obvious innuendos. I reverted to drink and eventually the banana leaves were spread on the table and a remarkably tough chicken stew served on it. 'I am sorry', said Antonio. 'They will be very upset if you don't show some appetite'. Public school training came to my aid, and I ate my portion, helped down by still more liquor. At around 4 pm we left.

The four-hour journey uphill to Bogotá was a misery. The boys quarrelled, the dog growled and the politician said not a word. Indeed he had not said anything since we had first met. Our ladies also thought the day had been a fair waste of time, especially as we had to have the Land Rover stopped every half hour. I began to feel ill, and by the time we got to the hotel I felt very ill indeed, and remained so all night. At moments like these wives are supposed to show sympathy. But not Ronie. 'It was not something you ate, it was what you drank', she insisted. 'I ate the same as you and I am all right'. But I explained the responsibilities of my position. *The Financial Times* cannot be seen to be uninvolved. 'Nonsense!' she said.

14. The Pan-American Highway

It is possible to jump into a taxi in Santiago, Chile, and be driven north almost to the frontier of Panama, where the Pan-American Highway peters out. It starts again the other side of the Panama Canal. Why the highway has never quite been finished, I don't know, because the gap is comparatively short, and easily completed with good modern techniques. Perhaps the Panamanians wish to keep the Ecuadorians or Colombians out. In 1973 when I was in Lima, I was offered the opportunity of driving south to Chile down the highway and grabbed at the chance. The purpose of the trip was twofold. I had been looking into land reform throughout South America and at the related problems of food supplies for the more deprived inhabitants, of whom there are a great many, in those parts.

The FAO runs a number of projects throughout the world to supplement local diets with food from the richer countries. I had seen some of these in Colombia and in Lima itself. At the time of this visit the supplies were from the main food surpluses, donated or sold very cheaply under aid programmes. They did not seem to be particularly well organised to me. For instance, stacks of dried egg powder from Britain, but no instructions how to use it. I sent a cable home to the Ministry of Agriculture for recipes to be sent. There were large administrative offices, but little evidence of any real impact on the obvious problems of nutrition, which were due to social inequality.

In fact, a distinction should be drawn between crisis food supplies, sent in answer to a natural disaster or one arising from war, and the general standard of supplies in the country concerned. The first is an act of God or the Devil. The second is, I am convinced, caused by the government of the country not doing its job properly. Therefore, while FAO and other organisations can provide the techniques, it is for the governments concerned to provide the resources to effect them. If a government is so inefficient as to be unable to feed and house its people, its inhabitants should change it. It is not for us in this anti-imperialist world to do the job for them.

The Peruvian Government of that time, 1973, was trying to improve things. It could best be described as a left-wing military dictatorship, determined to improve the condition of the ordinary Peruvians, of which there were and still are a great many. If I were going to reform South American agriculture I don't believe I would have started in Peru, because it is a most unpromising environment. The centre of population and industry is on the west coast where it scarcely ever rains. But a large population of Indians breed in the high Sierras of the Andes. There, thanks to modern medicines and hygiene, too many of them survive and have to emigrate to Lima and the coast, because the highlands won't support them. There in the slums, which I thought were even worse than those of Calcutta, they die off fairly quickly, but not swiftly enough to prevent a steadily increasing population bulge.

Because of the permanent drought on the coast, practically all agriculture is irrigated with water from the Andes and centred on rivers flowing into the Pacific. There is an enormous rain and snowfall on the Andes, but the bulk of it flows east into the Amazon Basin, where one day perhaps there will be more development. At present communications and climatic difficulties slow down all progress there, to say nothing of lack of finance.

I accompanied José, an FAO official, and his Swedish wife Christina on one of his inspection trips to see how the food aid was progressing. José was a Spaniard, a long-time FAO official though not very long in Peru. Christina was exactly what a Swedish woman should be, not austere and introspective, but blonde, luscious and not a bit dumb. I had my doubts about José from the start, or should I say about the whole FAO set-up. He drove us round Lima in a brand-new Mercedes. This, he said, was one of the perks of the job. He could, as a diplomat, import foreign goods like the Mercedes which were unobtainable in Peru, and after a couple of years sell them to local profiteers who were unable to import them legally. This was a well known diplomatic racket which the Americans had just stopped their officials indulging in. However, when we came to start the journey the Mercedes was replaced by an old Chevrolet belonging to FAO, together with a local driver. It would do the Mercedes no good, said José, to risk it on the country roads.

The coastal strip around Lima was originally settled by the Spaniards, who laid down the irrigation channels which are still operated by the original title deeds. There had been some land reform which I wanted to have a look at as well. On a previous trip I had visited a dairy farm on the outskirts of Lima with a thousand cows all milked by hand, zero grazed on maize, silaged and green. There was a brand-new rotary milking parlour on this farm, but having installed it the owner had funked starting it up. The milkers were all Indians and were milking in open sheds in extremely hot dusty conditions, but everyone seemed fairly happy. This farm had been reformed, I was told, and belonged to the workers, but the time was not yet opportune to visit it. As we passed it on the road it looked much the same as it had five years before.

Even on the outskirts of Lima the difference between irrigation and the lack of it was sudden and sharp. There would be a nice expanse of housing with gardens, orchards and green crops, then a desert where the owner had failed to tap the water channel. These coastal deserts did have some vegetation – dried-up plants and bushes – evidence of some moisture from drizzle and fog, but the further south we went the less vegetation there was. Eventually we drove through lunar landscapes where nothing had ever grown.

Our first port of call was near Pisco, the source of a well-known aperitif. At the land reform offices there we had a sight of the process in action. A very angry man walked in, obviously a landowner by the cut of his clothes, and complained long and vehemently about the way his land was being taken from him. The official he was haranguing said nothing until he had run out of breath, then produced from under his desk a copy of the land reform law, opened it and underlined some passages and handed it over. 'Take it home and read it,' he said, 'and then if we have done anything which was not according to the Government decree, come back again.' Shouting angrily '- - - robbers', he stamped out.

I asked the chief of the land reform if he had had much trouble implementing the new rules. He had previously been an adviser. No, he told me, the Government came from the same class as the larger landowners, and for the most part they were only taking land which had been unexploited or had a record of exploitation of the workers, or had belonged to foreigners or absentees. This seemed to be so. I met a number of smaller landowners later who did not seem to be too worried, though, as I was accompanied by officials, they might have thought it politic to say nothing.

The first farm we visited was growing maize and cotton, and was being run by a workers' committee. These had been the old workers on the place and they expressed themselves well satisfied with things as they were. They were organised in a co-operative, and the chief foreman was the man who had held the job before. The state of the crops was first class, and the farm was obviously under very firm management.

Co-operatives were not universally popular, so I asked if they had heard of the riots at a big sugar-growing co-operative in the north of the country. Yes, they said, they had heard of them, but they thought that the workers there did not appreciate the benefits co-operation could bring them. Was the farm as well farmed as it had been under the old ownership, I asked. It had been well run before but 'we are happier now that we have all the profits'.

As the farm had only been taken over a year or so before, I asked if they had had any material benefits yet. They apparently had compulsory schooling for their children, and a better water supply already. The old employer used to insist that children must put work before school. It all sounded too good to be true, but as I travelled further through the country I found that the Government's measures in this direction were meeting with a fair degree of approval.

Near Pisco we had a look at another FAO project, a compounding plant. The object of this exercise was to persuade the Peruvian farmers to grow their own cereals for pigs and other animals. The FAO's hand in this was to provide sorghum to mix with local supplies. Sorghum would certainly grow on the irrigated deserts but the costs of importing it seemed very high. At that time the world price for this grain was about £20 per tonne on board ship in the US but the delivered price to Pisco was over £60 per tonne. Someone somewhere was making a very good thing out of it. The farmers who came to collect the compounds appreciated the sorghum which was sold to them at a heavily subsidised price, but those I spoke to did not seem to think it would beat maize which was their main cereal ingredient.

Beyond Pisco the road followed the coastline, every now and then passing one of the fishmeal factories. These must be among the dreariest places in the world with no green thing at all. Simply a jetty, some rusty corrugated iron sheds, stacks of fishmeal in bags, some dilapidated trawlers and a disgusting smell of fishmeal over all. This was a most important Peruvian industry at the time, much encouraged by the FAO. Its basis were great shoals of anchovies which travelled up the cold Humboldt current. For many years they seemed an inexhaustible resource, but then suddenly they disappeared, leaving a comparative dearth behind.

There are two explanations for this. The most popular is that the

A butcher's shop in a country town, Columbia.

A village restaurant, Columbia.

Smallholders winnowing grain, Columbia.

Columbia – coffee beans coming into the depot on mule back.

current which brought the shoals moved further out to sea and made fishing very difficult. One day, the optimists claim, the currents will change back again, and catches will be resumed. The pessimists hold that the cause of the decline is over-fishing and that a return is far from certain. Strict fishing quotas have been enforced by the Government, but in spite of this catches don't seem to have increased as they should. Perhaps the first theory is the best. Fortunately for the world's protein supplies the decline in the anchovies was matched by expansion of soya bean production, which would not have made the strides it did, had the huge fishmeal supplies been available. One day the anchovies could come back and then there could be some cheap protein around again.

These anchovies had had a great effect on European agriculture before. They formed the food of a multitude of sea birds, and their droppings, accumulated and dried out over the ages, formed the basis of the first imported manures, the guanos. Some 300,000 tonnes were exported annually in the 1840s, and before they were exhausted some 10 million tonnes had been exported from one group of islands alone, mainly to Western Europe. The birds were still there in their countless millions, endlessly patrolling the shores. The rocks were white with their droppings. Guano mining is no longer practised, so no doubt these will become valuable as the ages pass.

It is an incredibly austere shoreline, dark grey cliffs and stony beaches with bright sunshine and the masses of birds. The Andes here are too far inland to be seen. Every now and then the road dipped into a river valley, and wherever this happened there were attempts at farming. In one valley someone had planted an enormous number of olive trees. They appeared to be thriving, but there was no one around at all. In another valley, a dry one this time, fields had been made and cotton and maize planted, but then the water must have failed and all that remained were the dessicated plants. I couldn't tell how long they had stood there, rattling in the evening breeze.

Approaching Arequipa, we crossed a plateau with some surrealistic shapes of driven sand like sharply cut quarter moons. Here nothing grew at all. Even the valleys the roads crossed were without water. There were some steep gulleys, and every now and then we passed little shrines with white crosses and inscriptions, memorials to those who could not keep to the road. There was very little traffic. Most of the transport is still by sea or air, or even by the railway, which runs much further inland. But there were taxis and some had come from Santiago, 2,000 miles to the south. There was the odd filling station and snack bar, garish with Coca Cola signs. I could even drink the stuff in that dehydrating country.

A few miles north of Arequipa, we arrived at an oasis. Not with palms as in Africa, but a square billiard table of an oasis, dotted with houses and buildings laid out with military precision. This was a new land reform settlement, a dairy farming complex where some hundred or so settlers were building up their herds under a very firm and very practical management. It was a co-operative, of course, but one where, it seemed to me, the members knew their places. The cattle used were Friesians, originally Holsteins, but they had recently imported a number of the Dutch cattle directly from Holland.

The job was well done and the cattle looked well. Their yields were as good as one could have expected in that sort of set-up where there is always doubt about the amount of compound feed needed. The individual farmers were keen on their work. I asked the director how he had come to secure such a high standard of settler. They were selected, he told me, from landless peasants who had never been on their own before. They had tried recruiting smallholders who might have known something about farming, but found that they were too independent, too accustomed to taking days off to go to market and fairs, and getting drunk. The settlers under his charge may not have known anything about farming, but they did what they were told, and appreciated the good housing and regular incomes they were now receiving.

How long would it be, I wondered, before the model farmers here began to be tempted to do as other independent farmers do the world over. How long before one peasant, more acquisitive than the rest, began to take advantage of his simpler neighbours. This was only a pilot scheme. There are moves afoot to divert one of the Andean rivers which is at present flowing east through the mountains, to provide the water for an enormous scheme. The land is there, it is level and of high inherent fertility. It could turn out to be as fertile as the valleys of California.

Near Tacna we set about tracking the whereabouts of cargoes of sorghum which no one had heard of for some time. There was said to be a mill at the local research station where it was supposed to be processed. The research station, probably built with overseas aid funds, was just as they are all over the world, with housing for livestock, laboratories and, more importantly, some quite nice housing for the personnel. Something had happened to the station, though. The mill which was supposed to be grinding the sorghum had obviously not been used for years. There were few cattle or sheep but there were a lot of guinea pigs. In fact, there was a research project on the creatures with trials for weight gains and food conversion.

Apparently the guinea pig is the main source of protein for the average Peruvian in those parts. Every kitchen, however humble, has a box of them alongside the stove into which are thrown all the scraps, and from which the Sunday joint or its equivalent is taken. Some of the animals were enormous, the biggest some 2 kg (4½ lb). That side of the business was certainly being well done. We never did discover what had happened to the sorghum. José shrugged his shoulders and said that it was in his predecessor's time.

We stayed a day in Tacna, and while there crossed into Arica in Chile to see if I could get a seat in a bus to Santiago or a taxi going that way. There was no chance, we were told. It was just before the fall of Allende and everyone was holidaying on the coast and elsewhere. Those buses whose crews were not on holiday or on strike, were booked for weeks in advance.

The Peruvian Government has changed now. The Generals have gone, and the civilians have now taken over. I often wonder what has happened to the land reform schemes I saw there. In a way they seemed to be too good to be true. They were certainly the most efficient I saw in all Latin America, productive and well managed. But how well they dealt with the human factor in the long term is very hard to say.

15. Chile – Land Reforms that Failed

I was in Chile a few months before the revolution ousted Allende, the first elected Marxist leader in South America. It was an extraordinary period. The whole of the previous social order was breaking down. Inflation was raging, unemployment rising, and shortages of everything were growing. There was very little if any violence, apart from the forcible take-over of a few farms by groups of activists. All other take-overs, not only of farms but of businesses and everything else, were by due process of law. These laws had been enacted by the previous social democratic governments, reforms for which the majority of the population had voted. But the system was clearly not working, so in the general exasperation of shortages and irresponsibility, the military took their chance.

Allende's government was not a Communist government, though it contained a few Communists. It was a well-meaning amalgamation of left-wing theorists of no executive ability. A real Communist dictatorship would not have stood for the all-pervasive inefficiency and irresponsibility, which was making life impossible for an increasingly broad spectrum of the population. Therefore when the military struck they had a far greater measure of support than they would have had earlier.

The Chileans had had a reputation for democracy and a democratically elected government for many years. How sad then that Allende's government had to be corrected by violent change by an impatient gang of generals. The killing of Allende was completely out of character with the usual run of Latin American revolutions, as the defeated president normally goes into exile.

Land reform had been one of the keystones of previous administrations, particularly that of Frey of the Social Democrats. The reason for its popularity was that much of the land was held in quite large units, and as there was very little industry to occupy the increasing population, it looked as though there should be room for some on the land.

I had visited Chile before. There was not the abject poverty of the Indians further north. The Indians I saw were the Auraucanians of the south, a people who had never been conquered by the Spaniards and lived in rather squalid independence on land which they had secured and farmed after a fashion, spending much of their earnings on drink.

The bulk of the population, rather like that in Argentina, were of European origin. But for some reason they seemed to lack the fierce independence that distinguishes the Argentinians. This was particularly true of the farm workers, who took a most servile attitude to their employers, so different from the men I used to work with on the other side of the Andes. If I had ever addressed the men I was in charge of as these Chileans were spoken to, I would have had a knife in my back in no time. But the Chileans seemed to take it with humility. Many of the farm workers were what were called Inquilinos, men living on the farms almost as serfs, according to some critics. They were in fact workers living in tied houses and had all the difficulties of moving away that tied cottage people do in Britain today.

Chile is not even a particularly good farming country. Much of the north and south is either desert or rain forest, but in between there are some hundreds of miles of well watered temperate land. This area is in the same latitude as New Zealand and the vegetation is much the same. It is good grass and arable land, and very suitable for temperate farming. Much was settled in the last hundred years or so after the last of the Indian wars, and the settlers were largely of European origin.

The country could be as productive as New Zealand, but because of an accident of geography, Chile is worse served by communications than almost anywhere else in the world. Most food production is for the home market, which does not generate sufficient cash for the development of highly intensive farming. But at the same time Chile's problems are in a way worse than those further north. The population is rising and the densest population is in the temperate region where heat and good clothing are needed to survive. It is easier to be really poor in the tropics.

The farm reform, or take-over, had been going on for a long time. Anyone with more than some 50 hectares of irrigated land, or 200 of dry cultivable land, was at risk. In practice though, those who had their farms taken legally were men with multiple holdings. Absentee owners also suffered, as did those who had other interests. Land which was not being farmed well was also at risk. There were also a number of illegal seizures. These erupt all over Latin America from time to time where activists don't consider reforms are going fast enough. I asked the then Minister of Agriculture, a Señor Chanchol, why the Government, which had the police and army on its side in those days, did not stop the seizures and chase out those who had taken the farms. 'We are not a repressive government', he said. That was what brought about the end of Allende.

I attempted to visit one of these farms that had been taken over, but was stopped at a barricade at the gates by a handful of students armed with pistols, who did not think *The Financial Times* could be interested in their goings on. They did not like my companion, a local landowner, either. So I visited three farms which had been taken over legally, as a guest of the Government.

The first was not far south of Santiago. I gathered it had belonged to a rich man who was still living in the house, and was now being run by the previous workers, the Inquilinos. They had certain advantages when it came to taking over land. The Government in its innocence imagined that land reform would help absorb some of the many thousands of rural unemployed. But they were gravely mistaken. The rural workers were divided into three main classes – the Inquilinos, who were permanent employees, the seasonal workers, and the unemployed. It was hoped that as a result of the reform these three classes would amalgamate on the farms and so remove the rural problems at a stroke. Not a bit of it. The Inquilinos were just as good at arithmetic as anyone else and could see that the fewer there were on a farm to share the profits, the more each would have for himself. So they just refused to take in the others.

When I was there, then, there were still just as many rural poor. Officials I met, mainly town-bred Marxists, deplored this in no uncertain terms. When I told them that it was simply good capitalistic common sense adapted to Marxist circumstances, they could not see the point – or the joke. I was rather sorry for those running this farm – a young man who had been born there and a sort of manager put in from the outside by the land reform agency. Neither of them knew much about practical farming, which soon becomes obvious if you ask the right questions. Farming there consisted of dairying with vines and fruit. So far it was carrying on under the previous management's impetus, which had been of a high order. But the workers I met seemed to be drifting around in a state of confusion. They did not know the first thing about the business of farming, and could hardly understand that they were now members of a co-operative farm. But they had not had time to let the farm drift into real chaos.

The next farm we saw, some hundreds of miles further south, was very different. We called at the local reform offices in the town, where we received a harangue on the beauty of land reform which even upset my very left-wing guide, who said to me, 'These men know nothing. They are political appointees'. If they had known anything they would not have taken us to the farm we visited. This was a biggish place growing cereals, including rice, and milking about 150 cows. The arable farming was in a terrible mess. Weeds were growing through the rice and wheat and the irrigation was not working properly. But the cows were even more of a shambles. They had a fine new milking parlour, a herringbone with good yards. But they were milking by hand in a row of hovels along one side of the yard because the electricity had not yet reached them.

'Where is it?' I asked. 'Just there'. They pointed to a pole which stood within 50 yards of the cowshed. 'Why is it not connected, then?' 'Because,' they said, 'we are not making sufficient money.' 'Why is that?' I asked. I was talking to them alone by that time, as my guides had drifted away in the face of growing hostility, and I speak quite reasonable Spanish. 'Because no one who comes here will tell us how to grow crops or how to sell them.' 'No saben nada', they reiterated. 'They know nothing'. It was a really tragic situation and bound to end in failure simply because the men did not know how to farm without reasonable guidance and co-ordination.

Only one of the farms I visited was really well run. This had belonged to a German who voluntarily handed it over, remained in the house and ran it as before, except that the workers now owned it and enjoyed the profits. He had been compensated as in all legal take-overs and did not worry very much. He had obviously been a good boss and his ex-employees appreciated him.

I have not revisited Chile for some years, but I understand the legal take-overs have stood. They were not forcibly restored to their previous owners, though if they were so minded, they could buy some parts of the properties back again. Some of the co-operatives are still working but most of the workers became individual smallholders and inevitably some of them began to buy out the less able.

But farming in Chile has not been much good of late. One of the first things the new government did was to destroy the system of subsidies and tariff protection enjoyed under previous governments. Farmers have had to take world prices, which has made things very difficult indeed for those of them that still remain. A friend of mine was growing sugar beet in a big way, but when world price sugar, including some from the EEC, was dumped in Chile, the local price collapsed and the factory closed. He was not allowed to dismiss any of his Inquilinos either, though he tried. They are better off than many others.

Chilean land reforms failed because the politicians of whichever party enacted them did not take a practical view of the difficulties that would arise. They did not see that in temperate agriculture economic progress depends on low labour and intensive cropping. Remember, the independent farmers in Europe evolved from the mass of peasants existing at the beginning of the Industrial Revolution. Factory work was the solution to rural poverty and over-population. But in many South American countries there is little if any industry in the Western European sense. Dividing the farms and estates into myriads of smallholdings is no solution. It can offer no more than an existence to those who live on them with no hope of a future at all. The politics of land reform are attractive for those seeking power. But they would not offer it so gladly if they had studied what happened in Mexico.

16. Mexico – Too Many Mouths to Feed

Mexican farming has two significant facets – large-scale land reform, and the development of the miracle wheats and maize of the Green Revolution. If land reform had been 100 per cent effective, there would not, in fact, have been a Green Revolution. But we will come to that in a while.

For nearly 50 years, until the third decade of this century, Mexico had been plagued by a succession of bloody revolutions. This is not the place to go into the causes of this endemic instability which affects all of Latin America to a degree. But the Mexican expression was particularly violent. Eventually the revolution wore itself out and among the pledges which the victorious party honoured was a commitment to land reform. This in itself was an extraordinary development, for few politicians in any part of the world have been known to keep their word once in power.

Land reform fragmented the farming of much of the country into hundreds of thousands of tiny holdings. The process was called the Ejido system, which took the place of the large-scale farming which had preceded it, on estates run, by all accounts, on almost feudal lines. The maximum holding was about 4 hectares, and a great many were a good deal smaller, depending on the quality of the land and the population of the area. At the beginning everyone was fairly happy. There was peace after half a century of war, and the population was still fairly small. But in the absence of continuous killing and instability the population rose alarmingly. At the same time the expectations of those on the land rose too. Many of the holdings had been laid out without thought of irrigation or even land quality, and could not provide sustenance, let alone an economic living, for many of the peasants.

So the surplus population began a drift to the towns, which is continuing today, as it does throughout most of Latin America. Outside Mexico City, and every other town, great and small, can be seen the dreadful slums into which these refugees from the country pour. A quarter of a million every year into Mexico City alone. There they exist in absolute destitution, a breeding ground for crime, disease and everything evil. Driving through these shanty towns is an appalling experience, made the more so by the knowledge that conditions there are better than in the villages they have left. Those who laid out the Ejido system may have been quite right when they allotted 4 hectares of land to a couple as a base for subsistence living. But after a couple of generations and improved hygiene the 10 acres might have to support two or three families with all their children.

It is estimated that 30 per cent of the Mexican population of working age is unemployed. By the year 2000 the population of the country will have risen to 100 million and this will mean 30 million out of work. What does one do about that? Birth control is an easy answer, but extremely difficult to organise in a Catholic country – or even a Protestant one. It is an appalling problem made worse in the visitor's eyes because this huge population appears to be set down in a particularly barren country. Where and how will they be able to eat, and what will they do with themselves? One of the problems of the Ejido system is that the individual peasant has had little opportunity to learn the skills of farming and marketing, or even how to keep out of debt. He is at the mercy of the merchant and moneylender, but he has one safeguard. It is difficult for him legally to dispose of his holding.

Popocatapetl is a volcano some 50 miles south of Mexico City. Before the all-pervading smog covered the capital it was possible to see its snows from the centre of town. The soil on the mountain slopes is good and there is irrigation water. It is also very much an Ejido settlement, with literally hundreds of very small holdings. One group of them had been organised by the Rockefeller Foundation, which has long been active in Mexico, into a semblance of modern farming practice. The theory of this particular project is to instruct the peasants in farming skills, in such a way that they can increase their yields within the limit of their own resources.

I spent the day with one of the Rockefeller advisory men, Jaime Garcia. He was, he told me, one of the children of a smallholder in an Ejido, and he had been fortunate enough to go to school and, what was more important, work his way through to the university. After graduating in Mexico he got a scholarship to the States and studied farming in California and elsewhere until he was recruited by the Foundation to join the team working on an Ejido near Puebla. The Foundation were insistent that those in contact with the local smallholders should be

Mexicans themselves, if possible from similar backgrounds.

On the way to the village he showed me the old hacienda which belonged to the landowner who had been dispossessed. It had been a fine colonial mansion but was now no more than a ruin, as were the buildings and irrigation works around it. One of the problems left by the revolution was that the land was cut up arbitrarily into plots. The map makers made no concessions at all to houses, buildings and natural boundaries or even the availability of water. The members of the Ejido lived in the villages, few had houses on their holdings and had to walk to and fro to work every day, sometimes for quite long distances. They were also completely ignorant of modern agricultural techniques. Where they had worked on the haciendas, the management had been entirely in the hands of the owners and their stewards. They just did what they were told.

The main crop on these volcanic slopes is maize. Maize has been grown for thousands of years in these parts and in fact the crop originated in Central America. But the varieties grown were very low in yield and subject to disease and pests as well. Many of the strains used had been grown for centuries. It was not until the Wallace family began to hybridise maize that there was a breakthrough in yields in the US, which has spread to many other countries across the world today. Hybrid maize is the result of the selective crossing of different strains, and the seed is only viable when it is the outcome of the first cross. This means that the hybrid maize company is guaranteed a market for ever. No one can grow a second generation from the first cross without risking a poor result.

The fact that the seed had to be bought, immediately made it essential that the smallholders developed a money economy – became real farmers, in fact. This is what Jaime and his colleagues set out to do. It was easy enough to persuade the smallholders of the benefits of hybrid maize seed with a few demonstration plots. It was harder to persuade them that cultivation and fertilisers were just as important. This is all elementary. But where this scheme parted from most others of this sort was a complete refusal to use the modern tools of husbandry. They used no tractors or other mechanised tackle. These, they reasoned, would be out of reach of the average smallholder's purse. So by example they were shown how and when to cultivate and sow their maize using the tools and resources they already had. This meant that the farmers were able to devote all their resources to growing maize, buying seed and fertilisers. But there also had to be a market for the surplus maize being grown beyond that needed for subsistence. To avoid the exploitation of the farmers by the merchant interests that always thrive in these situations, co-operative selling and buying had to be introduced.

During the day I spent at the settlement several things became very clear. The most important was that without the constant guidance of the Foundation's officials it was certain that exploitation by the merchants would probably keep them in deep poverty, as it does in India, for instance. This would in the end force them to reduce investment in seed and fertiliser and so the holdings would decline back to their primitive state again. It was very evident that the farmers appreciated the help from the Foundation officials. They trusted them and told me that without their help every man's hand was against them. Rural areas, they said, received the least in grants and help from the authorities. Education and medical services were at their lowest. The chances of many children escaping from the confines of a rural village, as Jaime had done, were infinitesimal. Despite his help, there was a constant threat of exploitation by merchants and moneylenders, and there was no really sound marketing organisation for what they produced.

Worst of all, the holdings were too small for their families to do anything but emigrate to the towns once they grew up. In fact, as one man told me, the situation had been made a bit worse because more of the children born survived than before improved farming came to them. I asked one man what they had to hope for. Would it have been better to leave the land in big blocks as before the Ejido system came into effect? 'That, no', he replied. 'We are at least free men. We can think and speak as we feel and we can listen to Cuba on the radio.'

It was brought home to me strongly that these peasants were not, as in so many of the developing countries, members of the coloured races who had been exploited for years. Most were of almost pure European descent, mainly Spanish, a fertile breeding ground for the more extreme forms of militant action to redress their wrongs. The only bar to this, I felt, was the memory of the revolutions. La Matanza, the killing, they called it, which had devasted the country for half a century. But the memory of these appalling times would eventually die. Meanwhile the injustices in Mexican society would grow and grow.

As a contrast to the Puebla project I then visited the other main Rockefeller enterprise in Mexico. This was CYMMIT, the institute for the development of maize and wheat. In brief, soon after the war the Foundation had decided one way to improve the living standards of developing countries would be to raise the productivity of their farmers. At least enough to provide them with sufficient food for their populations to eat. They concentrated their efforts on rice, maize and wheat, all crops to be grown in sub-tropical areas where the main populations of the world's hungry are to be found. The whole enterprise came to be known as the Green Revolution, and there were some spectacular successes, particularly with rice and wheat.

The problem with wheat was to develop a strain which would survive in a sub-tropical environment, and at the same time be able to respond to irrigation and nitrogenous fertiliser. The main man in charge for the Foundation in Mexico was Dr Norman Borlaug, an American of Norwegian descent, and to my mind one of the greatest practical farmers I have ever met. Borlaug did not breed any really new varieties of wheat. He did not have long enough for this. Instead, he selected from known varieties of dwarf or short-strawed wheats and crossbred them until he secured a number which would stand up to the conditions found in many of the countries in the tropical belt. The results were spectacular. In most countries where they have been established production has risen. In India wheat output doubled in a few years. The same principles applied to other crops also pushed up food grain yields.

Borlaug's work has on the other hand been attacked for making the farmers using the new systems become slaves of the capitalist system. Mainly because they needed fertilisers and other resources and like the Ejido peasants would no longer be self-sufficient. This is perfectly true. But surely it is better to find a system which will at least prevent people dying from hunger at whatever cost in giving up the simple life so beloved by the opponents of improved farming. I just cannot understand the philosophy of people who would seek to deny any country the advantages of extra food production because the methods used conflict with their own ideas.

I had met Norman Borlaug on previous visits to Mexico City but on this occasion flew up to the north-west of the country to the Yaki valley and the town of Ciudad Obregon, where he had his field headquarters. The Yaki valley had escaped the consequences of Ejido for the simple reason that until the building of a dam it was no more than a desert where the only farming was very extensive ranching. The dam completely altered the situation and immediately a very large acreage became available for irrigation. There was still some limitation of land owning. No more than 100 hectares of land were supposed to be held by any one man, but by bringing in all the relations it was possible to amass a fairly extensive holding suitable for capital investment.

The results were indeed spectacular. I was there in May, harvest was in full swing and the crops on the experimental farm and on the neighbouring farms were all very good. The main crop was wheat but there were also crops of safflower and oilseed and some of the wheat land was to be planted with soya. But there is no doubt that much of the success with the wheat was the result of its being cultivated on a large scale. The neighbouring holdings were of several hundred hectares at least, the mechanisation was complete and employment on the scale one would expect with mechanised farming.

This point has been seized on by the opponents of the Green Revolution and put to me time and time again. What is the point of developing large-scale farming and through its operation driving small farmers off the land and into the towns? It is a point that has recently been made by the locals of Ciudad Obregon and others in these reclaimed districts. There have been large-scale land seizures, and there is no doubt that though order is now secure, jealousy about land will erupt again and again. Thanks to the development of wheat in the Yaki valley, considerable prosperity has developed. There are flour mills in the town and a service industry for farming. None of these existed before, as there was just no farming. So the overall advantage to Mexico of more food, which was certainly needed, and some more employment, must definitely be a gain.

It is true that the valley could have been irrigated and cut up into countless smallholdings. But it is very doubtful if the overall production would have equalled what large-scale farming is securing. It is no good turning this land into blocks for subsistence farming. Irrigation in this context needs energy to work the pumps and the husbandry needs fertilisers, so a money economy is essential. Subsistence farming does not bring in money, and is a luxury that Mexico with its limited resources of arable land can ill afford.

Borlaug did emphasise to me though that he was only a technician. He had shown the Mexicans and others using his system how to grow wheat and other crops in the tropical belt. But he never claimed this was the answer to the world's poverty problems. At best, he said, the Green Revolution would keep food supplies just about level with demand for another 25 years. This was a breathing space, in which world governments would have to find ways of solving the problems facing them. This is a very tall order indeed, but one that must be faced. I do not believe that we in the Western nations have any responsibility for much of the misgovernment which is prevalent in many of these countries now. I have visited many of the key areas of the world's poverty and hunger, but in all these countries, even India, there are enough resources to feed and clothe all their citizens adequately, if only they are properly used.

The West cannot take over and run a sovereign nation, or tell its rulers they must not have an army or a national airline. That they must put in irrigation and fertiliser plants. At least it cannot do that without taking over power completely and at once reactivating the accusations of imperialism. This is not an abnegation of responsibility. There are ways in which these countries can be helped by means of trade and so on. But the basic choice of how a country's resources are used is its own responsibility.

The West is responsible for two very contradictory influences. On the one hand the Roman Catholics deplore and hinder the development of birth control for reasons which I frankly cannot understand. But then as an agnostic I cannot believe that any deity could possibly set out deliberately to condemn a society to persistent over-population with all the misery that brings. Every time the Pope insists that birth control by artificial means is a sin, then he and the whole of the Catholic Ethic lose credibility. There must have been a mistake in interpretation somewhere. Or else it could be understood as one way of increasing the Catholic proportion of the world's population.

Birth control would not have been needed though without the development of mass hygiene. As soon as the West becomes involved in the developing world, the malarial swamps are sprayed to kill the mosquitoes and elementary but effective sewage schemes are installed. Smallpox is now said to have been conquered and the outbreak of any plague is a signal for a mass attack on it with all the resources of the West. The factor which previously kept population down – i.e. disease – has been overcome, and even wars are generally nipped in the bud. I see no reason why the Catholics, often dedicated missionaries, cannot see this and do their best to help the authorities in these countries propagate population control. But this in no way abrogates the responsibility of individual governments to care for their populations. This is a tall order, but if it were made clear to them that nearly all the social misery of the developing world is really its own fault, they might begin to think about it.

PART 6: HOBBIES ON AND OFF THE HOOK

17. Salmon Fishing in Scotland and on the Wye

The River Shiel is one of the safest and most pleasant I have known – not more than a couple of miles long, draining the loch of the same name. Most, if not all the pools can be fished from the bank with the minimum of wading. At its head is the house pool, through which the river flows from a narrow passage through the rocks, cut at some early date, I suspect to lower the level of the loch. This narrow passage, the Gullet, is no more than 15 ft wide and through it has to come all the water of the Shiel catchment, sometimes in great volume. Up it swim thousands of salmon and sea trout on their annual return to spawn.

The Gullet is not easy fishing. The current is often too strong to allow the fly to sink and, except in the brightest sun, there is too much movement of the water to see if any fish are actually there, lying on the sill that forms the bed of the entrance. Fish are often caught there, but only on two occasions by me. The first time I was invited to go there by my friend Alastair, I was fishing the Gullet. Nothing happened when I was fishing in the traditional downstream way, casting across the current and allowing the fly to work in an arc.

When the sun came through I could see through polaroid glasses that salmon were lying on this shelf, but about 5 ft down, far below the passage of the fly. So, losing patience with the fish that refused to rise, I cast above them and allowed the fly to sink to the bottom of the run. This tactic worked within a few minutes. My fly was taken, and I caught my first Shiel salmon of about 11 lb. Once this had been landed and admired, I tried the same trick again. In a short while I could not lift the fly. It appeared to be stuck on the bottom, always a hazard in this sort of fishing. As I was trying to free it, the line began to move upstream. It was a very big fish and he took my line first up and then down the river. Then, when he had about 40 yds out, the hook came out. I never saw the fish.

After fishing the Gullet without success for the next ten years and, of course, trying upstream casting and other methods, I had another take. It was a horrible day with an upstream wind. I had been flogging the water for the best part of an hour when I decided to relieve myself. Because of the strength of the wind I had to turn my back to it, and to stop the fly blowing about I put down my rod and left the fly dangling in the water. Suddenly I heard the reel start clicking, but before I could turn round and grab it the rod was pulled off the rock on which it was lying. I saw it shoot straight out across the stream and into the pool. It was obviously a big fish, but again I never saw a sign of it. With my friends I searched the pool with a sort of grapple in hopes of snagging the line with the fish attached, but to no avail. Eventually the fish got free and the line floated to the surface. The rod was recovered the next day.

To say that I was mortified is hardly the word. I have never again put down the rod without keeping my foot on it, in case another miracle happens. Leaving the fly in the water while I have another rest is another tactic in my repertoire, but it will no doubt be another ten years before I hook another salmon in the Gullet. Not for want of trying though.

The moral of this seems to be that it does not matter how you fish for them, the fish are the masters because they only take the bait or fly in their own good time. Of course, salmon do not feed when they are in the rivers on the way to spawn, but they do on occasion take baits or lures which may have no relation to anything in nature. The average fly is but a streak of light to them, I think. But why do they take for just one short period of the day or week? There must be some combination of conditions in their environment which suddenly makes them start chasing lures. If we knew what these were, salmon fishing would be easy. Some ghillies obviously know something of this. They often take no interest at all in the fishing. This is infuriating to those who have spent a year saving up for a week's fishing, only to find there is nothing doing, and that their conscientious flogging of the river is tolerated by a supercilious ghillie who prefers to sleep under a bush.

The whole proceeding is so uncertain, in fact, that I wonder why I persist with it. A friend once told me that he averaged three salmon a year with 15 to 20 days devoted to it, and I should think my score is a little less than that. For the last three years I have caught none at all on the Shiel, not counting the one that took the rod. This was at least a moral victory – or one for the fish. It is not as if there is any great satisfaction in playing them out to land them. Once the fish is hooked, the sooner it is pulled in and killed the better. Anyway, a salmon is nothing like as exciting as a good two or three pound rainbow trout. In fact, the bigger the fish the easier it is to land, as long as it is well hooked. The attraction is the very uncertainty. Of course, if you see a lot of fish jumping about you are more hopeful than if the water is running down without a movement on the surface. But often the most unlikely looking spots will yield a pull – and at the most unlikely time too.

I once took a week on the Scottish Dee with Gordon Newton. We stayed at a hotel called the Cambus of May, and on the Sunday evening when we arrived there were a couple of obvious fishermen in the lounge. They asked where we were fishing. The Monaltrie Water, we replied. Useless since 1910, when the course of the river had changed. They were much better suited, they told us. No one, it was inferred, took the Monaltrie Water more than once. The ghillies were not much more hopeful. Too little water, no run of fish, the weather too cold. It was indeed. But Gordon and I won their hearts by taking them to the pub at lunchtime instead of leaving them to fish in our place, a common practice, we understood. By the Wednesday morning we had caught nothing and Gordon had to leave at midday to attend a function in Glasgow. I said I would stay on the job and keep the ghillies at it.

The Dee is fairly narrow at this point and on the other bank was a lady who had arrived the night before. I watched her set up her rod, try one or two false casts and advance towards the water. Then she tripped and fell and the line disappeared in the stream, where the fly was immediately taken away by a fish which I must have covered a dozen times. She played it in and while she was recovering her strength I cast over the same area and caught another fish within seconds. From then on the fun waxed fast and furious and at the end of the day I had four fish on the bank and had lost another three. Gordon rang that night and I told him what had happened. Fired with enthusiasm, he said he would take the night train back to Aberdeen and would be fishing the next morning. He was back for breakfast and we fished for the next three days, but because the snow had started to melt and the river had flooded we saw no more fish and caught none either.

One of the rods we had met at the Cambus turned out to have been the late General Sir William Morgan. He apparently spent the whole of his time fishing for salmon, having started this fairly late in life. He began with the Tweed, following on with the Dee and so on through the season. But his real joy in life was the River Lochy, which runs out of Fort

William. The General had established himself there as manager of the fishing on the owners' behalf. This was an almost perfect arrangement which gave him at least a month's fishing a year and the right to allocate lettings. Gordon and I asked to be put on his list and after I had done him a small service he obliged. So for several years we fished the Lochy with one or two friends in September. The Lochy is a very different story from the Shiel. It can be a very hard fishing river indeed, liable to a very strong fast water and a nasty bottom for wading, being mainly composed of round pebbles about 6 in. in diameter. It is also highly dangerous and several people have been drowned there.

On our first visit I nearly came to grief myself. The ghillie, who always seemed to me to have a bit of a chip on his shoulder, probably because he did not like Englishmen, indicated a general line across the river along which I should wade, and then went off to join one of the other rods. I started out but before long found I was getting out of a safe depth and that the current was sweeping me towards deeper water. I was so green that I did not have a wading stick, nor had I learned the safety drill demonstrated by Hugh Falkus that in moments of stress in these circumstances one should lie back and float downstream to safety. I have not tried it myself yet, but as I am a good swimmer I should have confidence to do it. If you think about it, it seems to be common sense. This decided me to give up breast waders once and for all. As long as I stick to thigh waders I am bound to keep in the shallows, because I don't like a wet cold bottom and the middle of a Scottish river is no place for grandfathers. If I cannot cover a fish from the bank or from my depth, good luck to it!

Latterly I have been spending a fair bit of time attempting to catch salmon on the Wye. This is a fine river with the great advantage that it is no more than a couple of hours drive to the lower beats. It is heavily over-fished, of course, and since the 1976 drought has got gradually worse. I don't believe this dearth of fish has been caused by deep sea poaching or by the locals, but simply because the drought in that year wiped out the stock of parr and smolt which were developing in the streams of the catchment areas. These either dried out completely or became so low and stagnant that these small fish could no longer survive. This was not really apparent until 1979, when catches were very much down. There appeared to be a shortage in 1980 as well. However, during the spring of 1980, I saw large shoals of parr, so presumably by about 1983 there should be some good salmon fishing again. Or perhaps I should say that more salmon should be seen.

One of the features of the Wye fishing used to be the very large number of fish that could be seen jumping around or porpoising. This kept my enthusiasm at boiling point, even though I was catching none. But in 1979 and '80 there were hardly any to be seen anywhere, and there is no greater misery than fishing a river where there appear to be no fish. Although most beautiful, the Wye is in many respects a beastly and dangerous river. The banks are insecure, often with deep water close in, and some of the rocks are traps for the unwary.

I was once fishing near Llandogo and had actually hooked a fish and was playing it as best I could from a rather insecure stance among the rocks. I kept trying to ease it ashore so it could be beached, but the more I tried to move myself, the more I found that one leg was stuck between two rocks and just about at the depth limit of my waders. I twisted and turned while also trying to keep the fish under control, but to absolutely no avail. So I decided that instead of beaching the fish, I would bring it close enough to me to grab its tail and secure it that way. Salmon have a fin in front of the tail, and an experienced man can hold a fish by it. I was not experienced, but I had seen it done. I felt I was gradually winning, but then the inevitable happened. The fish swam round me and, relieved of the spring of the rod, the line tightened and the fish was able to get off. I staggered ashore, determined never to go fishing again without a gaff or net on my person. I had left it on the bank. When I had recovered my breath I found that my hip joints had seized almost solid, and for the next two or three weeks I was a virtual cripple.

I was once offered some very good water belonging to a friend just near Symonds Yat on condition I fished one day a week and gave the owner half the fish caught. But I had to pass an exam first to judge my suitability. It is a marvellous stretch of water with possibilities both for spinning and fly fishing. We embarked in a boat and started fishing. Geoffrey knows the Wye and how to catch salmon, and is a most methodical fisherman. Salmon, he kept telling me, have certain lies which have been there for generations, so casting had to be within very narrow limits indeed.

I found his insistence on fishing only the right spots, although undoubtedly founded on experience, rather boring. Particularly as if I did not drop the bait within 6 in. of an indicated spot there was a disapproving murmur. I like to be adventurous in my fishing, and try all aspects of the river. I spent two days with him but obviously did not pass the test because I was never asked again. I understood I lacked the application necessary to make the best use of a beat. Geoffrey was quite right, of course. The real skill, or should I say the right ingredient, for catching salmon is simple persistence and knowledge of the lies. Keep the fly or the bait passing in front of where the fish is lying, or where you think it is lying, and on one of the passes you will, if you are very lucky, be surprised by a sudden pull on the line. There is no real skill about it once you can throw a bait or cast a fly, which can be learnt on the lawn or in the local park. To go to the river as a novice, as I did, is a waste of time for salmon fishing or for any other sort of game fishing.

I have caught so few salmon that almost every one is memorable. One of the most exciting was on the Shiel. It was a marvellous sunny day and I was looking down from the road bridge into the river which was running fairly low. Upstream I saw a salmon lying about 10 yds from the bank, which I marked and decided to have a go from the bank. Then I saw three fish lying some 20 yds below the bridge in the gin-clear water. I suggested to Alastair, who has to use crutches, that if he came on to the bridge he might be able to drift a fly down over these fish. This was quite easy. The current was running straight down and the fly seemed to travel naturally. The first he put on was a Practitioner, a sort of artificial prawn. Real ones are forbidden on the water. The fish simply swam aside and let it go past. He then put on a slightly smaller brightly coloured fly, from which they really did shy away. Then I tied on a very small Hairy Mary which passed between the fish again. Suddenly another fish, which had been lying below them, swam up and took the fly.

Once it had been well taken, the salmon took out about 70 yds of line, then turned and dashed up under the bridge. Alastair wound in furiously and just managed to check it before it could turn round the pillars and so come off. He then gave me the rod so Chris, the third member of the party, who had been fishing downstream, could land it when I had played it out. This took some doing, as it was a very active fresh run fish and it was impossible to get below him to play him when the stream was against him. I always like to make the fish run upstream. Eventually I managed to pass him over Chris's net, but he missed it and the fish made off under the bridge again. I put great pressure on the rod, there was a loud crack and for a moment I thought my knot had come undone. But it was the rod, which had parted just above the bottom joint. The top three pieces slid down the line, caught the fish on the head and stunned it. It turned on its back and was easily scooped out. It weighed 15 lb.

Alastair is a great fisherman in spite of his disability and one afternoon managed to hook five fish. As I was nearest to him I had to land them for him, leaving my own rod some 50 yds downstream each time. There I had found a salmon which rose to me like a trout, something they seldom do.

The fifth fish was a monster and it took Alastair the best part of 20 minutes to get it close enough for me to gaff. When I got ashore Ali lay back exhausted. Then, when he had recovered somewhat, I noticed he was taking his pulse. 'Up to 150, John', he said. 'If it had gone any higher it would have been the end of me. What a wonderful way to go!' 'And how selfish can you get?' I replied. 'We still have two days of the week left and if you succumbed now we should not be able to enjoy them.' I went back and caught the fish I had been trying for when I had been interrupted, but from that moment until the end of the week I did not catch another fish, nor did anyone else.

I have a friend who has a farm on the Tweed and part of the tenancy is a beat of the river. I was staying with him at the end of November and he arranged for me to have two mornings fishing. He did none himself and let the rods. It was horribly cold weather and although I caught one fish I was glad when lunchtime came and I could decently retreat. The next morning I caught another and Robert took my rod while I went up to the house for a cup of coffee. When I came back he was into a fish, which he landed. Since then he has taken back three days' fishing and talks of nothing else. I always thought he was among the best farmers on the Tweed but the fishing does not seem to have done his farming any harm at all. If it had been my stretch of river, I don't believe I would ever have let any of it. But then I might have become bored.

The salmon fishing season in these islands is a long one. With a skilful choice of river one can be fishing somewhere every week of the year. I average a day a fortnight through the spring, summer and autumn. I set out with the greatest of hopes, and though I know I shall be most unlikely to catch anything, my imagination runs riot as I play out a succession of wonderful fish. Nineteen times out of 20 I am disappointed, but that does not stop me.

18. On Failing in Politics

My failure to secure a seat on the Hampshire County Council in 1945 was a turning point in my life. I had offered myself to the voters in the first post-war election and secured, if I remember rightly, 400 votes out of a total of about 1,500. I followed this defeat by offering myself to a more localised electorate for a seat on the Rural District Council and lost that as well – in the same year.

I was not only mortified, but angry that the electors did not see the value of the contribution I could provide in building the brave new post-war world. My opponents were the so called Independents, Conservatives to a man or woman, who were determined, whatever happened at national level, not to surrender the grass roots to the socialist menace. For I was standing in the Labour interest and had been a keen supporter of the Party for the last year or so of the war. The reasons for this were obvious. I had experienced the 1930's and had been particularly impressed by the sufferings of the unemployed and as indeed had almost everyone else in the deflationary climate of those times.

This mood was heightened by the Left Book Club's publications, the *New Statesman* and the propaganda for a better world which had been published during the war. It seemed to me that only a Labour Party dedicated to changes for the better could be relied on not to plunge us back into the climate of the pre-war years. Like many others I could see no alternative to a Labour Party as a means of securing that improvement. Otherwise it might have been so much eyewash, designed to make us fight through to victory.

I was very upset by the privilege and unfairness which were a feature of British life between the wars. I was always being told that things were better than before the First World War. Possibly they were, but I did not see why someone should have his life made easy just because he had been born in a certain bed, while down the road another, born on the same day, should be faced with every obstacle to leading a decent life.

Such sentiments were deemed extraordinary by many of my neighbours, who felt that as an up-and-coming capitalist I should certainly not be on the Labour side. But I don't think there is any conflict at all in this. I have been happy to compete in the capitalist game, but I felt I could be an even more successful capitalist if I was operating in a fairly prosperous environment, rather than in the miseries of the 'twenties and 'thirties. So I joined the Labour Party and decided to take an active part.

To be a politician it is essential to be able to make a speech, but until the beginning of the war no violet was more shrinking than I. I would have dropped dead rather than open my mouth in public. But the Army altered that. I was sent to Woolacombe on a weapons training course for the Home Guard, where I was mixed in with a squad of NCO's and junior officers. Among the subjects taught was the Mills bomb. I can see the NCO instructor now. Gaunt and absolutely humourless in the flat-sided metal spectacles issued to be worn beneath gas masks.

Taking the bomb in his hand he would declaim, 'This is a Mills bomb. Its chief characteristic is its steep angle of descent'. Then he paused. 'Such as we hope for Herr Hitler. Joke, see! You must always drive home these points with a joke or telling anecdote.' As we were budding instructors we then had to repeat his spiel verbatim to the rest of the class in turn. After stammering through my piece a dozen times in front of the rest of the squad till I was word perfect, I didn't give a damn about anything, and have never stopped talking since.

In his simplistic way he was defining the principle of public speaking, which is to leaven the message with humour or a point that will keep the audience from going to sleep. I am firmly of the opinion that the human mind can only take in one thing at a time, and that it remains receptive for only a limited period. When I started broadcasting I was told four minutes was the maximum any mind could accept. Once I was having dinner with a judge who told me he had spent an hour and a half summing up in quite a simple case. 'Then you simply confused the jury,' I said, 'as I was confused when serving on one.' He was not amused.

Having been taught the skill, by numbers as it were, I became quite adept at it and found it was possible to sway quite large audiences to my way of thinking. Most of my speaking was at NFU meetings and I remember I once defended an unpopular price review backed by headquarters against a mass meeting of Hampshire farmers. It was really quite a performance. I promised them that should headquarters turn out to have let them down, I would be the first to assail them. In the event headquarters *did* let us down and I assailed them ever after. In this I was simply displaying the first rule of any political career which is to look after one's home base first, last and all the time. If carried to extremes as I did, this is not the way to high office, whether in the Labour Party, the NFU or any other elected body, where compromise and the possible are the criteria. But it is much more enjoyable.

Except for speaking at the celebratory rally after the 1945 election, the Andover Labour Party did not provide me with much time for hyperbole and excitement. The meetings were governed – no other word for it – by the Party's standing orders. Minutes had to be agreed before they were signed, every detail was hammered out, points of order, amendments and appeals to the chair were legion. The delegates from the Trade Unions were by far the most pedantic. It may be the democratic way, but it was damned dull to one like myself who wanted to change society, yet found he couldn't speak twice on a motion without being called to order.

Trade Unionists formed the core of the local party, with a sprinkling of cooperators and others, none quite like myself. We were advised that nothing should be done to help the Communists and one left-wing lady was only allowed to help our candidate after she promised not to advocate Marxism. But she maintained her rights and we agreed that she should continue to think in terms of dialectical materialism. What that meant, I have no idea.

I did a certain amount of canvassing on behalf of our candidate, but in Hampshire, particularly North Hampshire, there was simply not enough of an industrial base on which to build a Labour majority. Besides, our candidate was a woman, an excellent and kindly lady, but in the male chauvinist atmosphere of the time women candidates had to be superior beings indeed to succeed. Eleanor Rathbone, Lady Astor, Jennie Lee and Ellen Wilkinson were in a class apart.

I then stood for the County Council and spent some three weeks canvassing a rural area south of Andover asking people to vote for me so I could spend a good deal of my time working for them for no pay at all. I did not fight from my own home base as the local member was, though Independent, one of the few who were really independent, and it was thought politic not to oppose him. Nor would I be welcome in Andover itself where I might have won a seat – there were two at the time – because the trade unionists had candidates.

Canvassing for oneself is a most humiliating experience. Fancy walking up to the door of a perfect stranger and asking him to vote for you in the

Labour interest. The usual reply to my request was 'Why should I?' – a good question which I never found easy to answer. My opponent, a brother of Lord Selborne, saw to it that his supporters dominated such meetings as I held. In fact they were usually the only ones to attend. Feudalism was slow to die in Hampshire in the 'forties and people of the working class still feared for their positions if they were seen openly to support a Labour man.

I gradually lost interest in the Labour Party after this, though not from any decline in my sympathy with the basic ideals of a fair chance for all and better social services. I could have gone further. In fact, the then secretary of the Agricultural Workers' Union, A. W. Dann, asked me if I would consider standing for a reasonably safe Labour seat. By this time I had had dealings with Ministers and bureaucracy through the NFU, and wanted no more. This is, if you like, a confession of failure and selfishness, but I am not a compromiser. Nor could I stand for being a member of a council or public body which could not get rid of all its civil servants if it wanted to if they obstructed the will of their elected masters. This is most important. I believe the elected individual must be the boss in the last resort. It is the only fair way to assume responsibility.

I was once staying on a ranch in Colorado when a rather obsequious fellow dressed in the uniform of a cattleman – Stetson, tight jeans and high boots – drove up and accepted coffee. During the subsequent conversation it transpired that he was the local road surveyor. His term of office was coming to an end and he was standing for election in a few months' time. He asked if the roads had been kept to my host's satisfaction, and if any bridges wanted repairing and was obviously out to please. In Britain the local surveyor is a civil servant and even if, as in one town I knew of, he had mislaid the plans of the drains, necessitating wholesale inconvenient excavations to find them, he was still safe in his job. In the States, in Colorado at any rate, his job depended on satisfying his constituents. There is a lot to be said for the American system where most public officials are accountable for their actions and not, as in Britain, able to shelter behind their elected, but not really responsible masters.

I don't suggest that this country would have been any more prosperous or better governed if we had had direct elections for all sorts of officials above a certain level. But at least we should have had the satisfaction of knowing we had a hand in direct government and could alter things at the first shake of a ballot box much more directly than we can under the present system.

Some of my writings have been called political, a judgement I largely disagree with. I am not seeking to change governments at all. I back neither side openly – I preserve my independence. If in the Press I attack certain policies, it is the policies I am attacking, not the people pushing them, whom I believe to be honest but mistaken. I am seeking, not with great success I must admit, to make people in power change their ways. It is everyone's right to do this in a free country.

I was once viciously attacked at a dinner by a speaker who claimed that journalists like myself were, in Stanley Baldwin's words, just like harlots through the ages, who had all the power but none of the responsibility. I am sure I have never wanted any responsibility – no voter would ever give it me. And such power as I have had to change things has been minuscule and hardly enough to qualify me as a harlot.

19. Trout Fishing on Rivers Nearer Home

Let me say straight away that I am devoted to dry fly fishing because I enjoy it, not because it is a particularly skilful occupation. This statement is sacrilege, of course. Everyone has read endless descriptions of watching a fish rise, casting a fly delicately in its line of vision and then catching it. A great deal of nonsense is written about the skills needed to do this. They are in fact non-existent, or rather can be learnt in short order on a lawn or other open space well away from a river by anyone with the least skill and co-ordination between his eye and his muscles. Mind you, I did not know this at the start. I began to be interested some 30 years ago on the Kennet. I had done some wet fly fishing in Ireland and other places which consisted of casting a fly across the stream and letting the current carry it round. If the wind is behind you, it is very easy and there are streams where it is the only way. Salmon fishing is, of course, simply an extension of this technique.

The Kennet is a good trout stream and was in those days well populated with mayfly. This insect has a special characteristic on the Kennet, as it arrives in June. When it does the river is covered with insects from time to time, either hatching or dying. The fish feed ferociously on them. Equipped with rod and artificial mayflies I went to the river and started fishing. Now the trouble with the Kennet is that it flows from west to east and in June the wind always seems to be blowing from the west. I had never cast into the wind before, so for the whole of my first season the fly was blown about by the wind in every direction except near the fish. This was my first mistake. I should have spent my spare afternoons practising on the lawn against the wind, as I had been told. In fact using mayflies in these circumstances is even harder than using the smaller types. I was not much more successful for the rest of that season. There was very little interest from the fish once the mayflies had gone. So I never managed to catch fish at all the first year. But this did not destroy my enthusiasm, as it might have done.

The next year I attacked the river properly armed. I had practised assiduously for weeks on a field out of sight of scoffing neighbours and family, and could drop a fly with reasonable accuracy. On this occasion the Kennet hatch was terrific, with the river carpeted with fly. The fish were there all right. But there were so many fly to choose from that the fish never took mine. It would have been better to find a single fish looking for food in a stretch where there was not so much of a hatch. At length, walking upstream I found one opposite a garden on the other side. I put all my lessons into effect, cast the perfect fly and caught quite a nice fish. No sooner had I landed it than an angry gentleman appeared on the opposite bank and asked me if I realised that members were only allowed to walk up this stretch, that the water by his garden was only for himself and guests, and that this was the only fish in it. Don't you read the rules? I had to confess that I didn't.

I didn't do much better for several years. One reason was that the Piscatorial Society, to which I belonged, had many members much better than I was. Their casting was extraordinarily good and they seemed to know just where the fish would be rising. They were always sitting on these places from early morn till late at night. They guarded these sites with all the determination of the French at Verdun in the First World War. There is no real fellowship between competing anglers in a short mayfly season. If I did happen to come across a rising fish there was usually someone waiting to take my place after a few minutes, and I don't perform well in front of an audience. The line would get out of hand, the fly splash down, and remarks were heard about telling the Committee about people who only come to the river to scare the fish.

Increasing prosperity enabled me to move to the Test, that Mecca of dry fly fishing. By then I was at least competent at casting and tying on flies. I had had a preliminary canter there, and had been offered a day, election day 1955, in fact, when someone had had to forego his day because he was voting. It was, in fact, the best day for mayfly I have ever seen on the Test. I also had a high temperature, I discovered afterwards, which was to stop me fishing altogether for some time. The river was literally boiling with fish. But the beauty of it was that I was alone on my beat. There was no one to criticise, for there was plenty to criticise. I kept losing flies in bushes and trees and by the end of the day I was down to my last 3 ft of cast. But the limit in those days was eight fish and I had caught the limit, averaging just 2 lb each. I realised what I had been missing all my life and put myself on the waiting list immediately. In future all my responsibilities, and there were many at the time, would have to take second place to fishing.

The great thing about the Test is that it is a river where there is a hatch of fly most days in the year. At least it seemed like that. Also it is a river where, thanks to the clearness of the water, the trout can see those flies and rise to take them. This has always been so, and in the old days trout fishing on the Test was famous. The other factor is that, rising in the chalk, the Test, like other chalk rivers, does not have the spates and droughts which affect many other river systems. The chalk Downs act like a sponge, soaking up the moisture as it falls, then exuding it gradually throughout the season.

Near Stockbridge the Test flows through old water meadows on a peat subsoil. The water here is too acid to rear small trout, so most of the wild fish are bred in the smaller tributary streams, then navigate to the Test as they get older and tolerant of more acid water. There are very few natural fish, so the river has to be stocked with stew-fed fish, so that fishermen can be assured of reasonable sport. This artificial rearing is condemned by the purists, but I doubt if many of the critics have ever fished a part of the Test which does not contain some reared fish. Anyway, when I have fished the upper reaches of the stream, I have found the wild fish even more eager to take a fly than the allegedly tamer ones that come out of the stews. After a few days in the water the stew fish themselves develop all the cunning usually associated with the wildest fish.

Over the years I have developed a technique of my own. I have a theory that fish develop a taste for a certain fly which lasts for a season or two. It need not necessarily look like anything actually coming down the river at the time, because even the finest imitations are nothing like the real thing, or would not appear so to the knowing eye of a fish. The nearest an artificial fly can get is in outline and shape. I don't think colour has much to do with it, though a colourful box of flies pleases the fisherman. For instance, for several years I found a fly called the EAA was an absolute killer. This was a hackle fly – that is, it had no wings – and was mainly characterised by a rather thick body with a hump in it as if the creature was pregnant. I saw it in someone's box and it looked exactly right, so I had several tied for me. I fear I have neither the time nor the skill to tie my own.

When floating well it was taken at any time of the day, as long as the fish were moving. The reason it was so attractive, I thought, must be its resemblance to a nymph turning into a fly on the surface. But after three seasons when I filled my limit several times with it, the attraction waned and I could no longer count on its success. Today I never even put one on. Why has this happened? If Darwin's theory of evolution is anything to go by, the explanation would be that over the years the fish that succumbed to that fly would have been extinguished, as none would be left to breed. But this is clearly nonsense, so it must be that their appetites change, as many other creatures' do.

Since the EAA went out of fashion, I have reverted to a similar sort of pattern, a pheasant tail which is the same as the EAA but without the pregnant hump. In various sizes it works quite well. But whatever the fly pattern, its presentation is all important. It goes without saying that if you are dry fly fishing, the fly should float down to the fish which you have spotted, rising to the natural. Once you get to know the river well you know where fish are likely to be and where they are likely to rise. The hatching flies travel down the faster sections of the current and if there is much wind will be blown across to the windward as well.

But the surface of a big stream like the Test contains a great variety of currents, all running at slightly different speeds. If you cast your fly across this stream, ten to one the fly will be moved by the pressure of the water on the cast almost as soon as it has hit the water. This makes the fly act unnaturally, something the fish will always spot. This phenomenon is called drag, and overcoming it is a most engrossing task. It means unlearning all the books tell you about throwing a straight cast. This is all very well in salmon fishing or in casting on a reservoir, but on a living stream more is required. To avoid drag the line must fall on the surface in a zigzag pattern, so that as the fly floats down the stream the different pressures on the cast are balanced out, without imparting an unnatural drag to the fly. It took me a long time to work this out, but I found the best way to achieve it is to cast in the normal manner, then when the line is falling on the water to give it a sharp check or tug. This spoils the pattern of the cast but makes for a naturally floating fly.

Most rivers I fish with the dry fly have a rule which says that only upstream fishing is allowed. This is often difficult to interpret. Suppose there is a fish rising under a bridge at the bottom of your beat. It is obviously your fish. The next rod below will certainly never be able to reach it. But you can't fish it from below. The answer here is to let the fly float down to it. This does not mean downstream fishing as with a wet fly, but it means casting the fly so that it will float naturally on the surface on a very loose line so the fish will take it. I maintain that this is perfectly legal, as is fishing straight across the river to a rising fish on the other bank. A famous general, now deceased, whom I found doing this on my beat from his own next door, said that as long as his feet were in his beat and the fly was not being wet fished, it was all perfectly in order. One does not argue with generals, but only agrees with them.

Overcoming such problems is the great fascination of the sport to me. I don't believe the fish have the sharpness of vision and of hearing that people claim. In fact, I believe a feeding fish is only interested in eating as much as it can. It looks very professional to kneel behind a clump of rushes and cast from there, but I don't believe it is so important. For an elderly man kneeling on damp grass can lead to rheumatics! I was once fishing on the Kennet when I saw a rod a few hundred yards away signalling to me. This was an elderly doctor who had knelt to cast at a fish and found that he could not get up again. I got him to his feet and he staggered away. Now he was saved from a most uncomfortable evening because there were other rods about. But on the Test where I am alone on the beat, I would have to stay there until the search party arrived, if I ever got into that position.

Regrettably the Test is no longer quite what it was. The 1976 drought killed off a lot of the weed and destroyed much of the fly life. The weed has returned and there are still quite good hatches of fly, but for some reason or other the fish have been forgetting how to rise. In the latter half of the 1980 season a rising fish was quite hard to find. This was not confined to the trout but was true of the grayling as well. Others have noticed the same phenomenon, but I don't pretend to know the answer. It is true that fish never rise as well towards the end of the season, and then nymph fishing is allowed. The nymph, the fly as it leaves the bottom to rise to the surface, is fished below the surface and generally speaking upstream. Sometimes one can see fish taking nymphs, just sucking in the nymphs without breaking the surface, but I have found that such fish will usually take a floating fly if it's properly presented. The advantage of using a nymph in difficult water is that, being below the surface, it will not drag as a surface fly will, but I don't really like using it. It is all too easy to fish blind, just throwing the nymph in and sweeping the river as if wet fly fishing. There is no skill in that. It's just butchery.

Once you have the knack of putting the fly down on the water where you want it to land, and constant practice can make you reasonably good, it does not seem to matter how hard the fly comes down nor really what it looks like. But I will except the winged fly from this. They are designed to float down with their wings erect and when they lie flat on the water with their wings still at the same angle, I am sure the fish get suspicious. If your fly pitches down in a crumpled mess though, it is exactly what the fish expects most of the time. Most of the flies end up dead on the water after mating and the crumpled mess of hackled fly looks perfectly natural to me. Nor do I believe that fish are frightened by a splash. They expect dead flies to splash and anyway some of the fallen flies or spinners splash around quite a bit on the water.

As I have said, I don't think the skill required for dry fly fishing is in any way out of the ordinary. But the skills of modern coarse fishing are of the highest order. Coarse fishermen, however, go to the river to catch fish, weigh them and put them back again. They devote the most scientific techniques to preparing the bait, varying the rods they use, and so on. They are the real artists. I go to the river after dry fly to relax. I only have to take action after I have seen a fish rise to a natural fly or two. Otherwise I can sleep, go to the pub, or even, as I often do, write an article. Some of my best thoughts have come to me in quiet moments on the banks of the Test. Indeed, it is often a bloodless sport and I like it that way. That is more than I can say for my salmon fishing, which is often bloodless but much harder work.

PART 7: SOME OTHER VISITS

20. Israel – Have Rifle, Will Farm

I have been to Israel three times – in 1967 just before the June war, in 1969 and again in 1973, a few months before the Yom Kippur war. I don't think I shall go there again. My main reason is what I took to be the changing attitude of the Israeli people themselves. I simply looked at their farming and its economics. In 1967 the people I met were largely of European origin with whom I had a common bond, though few were English, French or American.

In 1967 the country was still in great danger. Jerusalem was divided and communications to the north and south were within range of light artillery along the coastal corridor. The burnt-out armoured lorries on the road up to Jerusalem were a memorial to the bitter struggle for survival 20 years before. I met many who had fought then, and honoured them as brave and dedicated people.

They lost no opportunity of reminding me of the danger of their position. At a kibbutz on the eastern shore of the Sea of Galilee they showed me the Syrian village, a few hundred yards up on the Golan Heights, from which a mortar attack had been launched in which the girl getting in the cows had lost her legs. I was standing on the very spot, they told me. Our driver guide provided by the Government had a Sten gun under his seat.

We asked the driver, ex-British Army, what Israel needed for peace. We were looking at a map on the bonnet of the car at the time and he answered without hesitation, better frontiers. A few months later in the Six Day War they had taken the West Bank and made the Jordan the boundary.

But in 1969 they were still in danger. I was making a film of the farming and was taken to other spots where we could have been shot. On one occasion we had a drive down the frontier with Jordan. We had an armoured car escort, whose crew put on their helmets and loaded their rifles as we approached the frontier. Being in an ordinary car I felt very vulnerable.

At that time the Suez canal was the scene of constant shelling and the only outlet to the Arab world was the Allenby Bridge which carried the road to Jordan. We filmed Syrian grain coming over the border, the sacks being bayoneted in case an infiltrator had hidden in them. I felt very vulnerable doing my piece 'to camera' in front of the Israeli machine guns, which were at my feet. I could sense the Jordanians behind me, though I could not see them.

Later, on the road back to Jerusalem, we stopped to film some Arab shepherds who were living in some nearby caves. One of the men looked very unlike a shepherd, with polished shoes, and kept his face away from the camera. While we were filming, there was a sudden outbreak of small arms fire from the direction of the bridge, which went on for some time. The next morning in *The Jerusalem Post* I read that security forces had raided caves along this road and lost several men in a battle with infiltrators.

During the course of this trip I met several Arabs, some in quite good positions, who told me the Israelis were treating them well. They were indeed classed as Israeli citizens, but each told me that deep down they knew they could not be anything but Arab. They looked on the Jews as enemies who would have to go. These were not West Bank Arabs.

Even more interesting was the attitude of some of the settlers in the farms. One or two told me they realised that the areas where they had settled had belonged to someone else. There were the remains of homes and fields there and they worried about it. No doubt the constant threats to their security accentuated this feeling.

By 1973 all that had changed. Security was much better, there was no activity on the Suez Canal and the Israelis I met, again when filming, this time the country's water supplies, were almost contemptuous of the enemies beyond their frontiers. Security was so lax that my luggage was not even checked at Tel-Aviv airport. Two days afterwards some Japanese terrorists caused a minor slaughter there. This was rationalised as being no more than a dying effort by allies of the Palestinians, who were unable or unwilling to risk their own skins.

Nowhere was this complacency more apparent than among our film crew. John Kenyon, my producer, and I were for the second time making a joint BBC Israeli film. On both occasions the crew were local. On my first visit they had all been of direct European origin. On the second all bar one were locally born, though of European descent. They spoke mainly Hebrew and had very little English or any other European language. It was very difficult to find common ground with them. They had different values.

But the culmination of my disillusion came when filming on a large kibbutz in the Negev desert near Beersheba. Irrigation had undoubtedly made the desert bloom and I asked the man in charge who had been there before the kibbutz had been set up. 'Nothing and no one', he said. I persisted, 'Really no one?' 'Nothing, I tell you. Only Beduin.' Rather as if he were talking of rats.

I had a small revenge as we made our crew film various aspects of elementary Beduin farming, and in the commentary of the English version pointed out that the Israelis had had the advantage of enormous capital gifts from their sympathisers. No doubt the Beduin could have done as well, had they had the same resources. I don't know if this was left in the Israeli version.

As it turned out this contempt of the Arabs brought about by three or four years of peace nearly cost the Israelis their country. They only saved it with heavy losses in the 1973 war. Although invited back to make another film, I felt I had to refuse. However impartial my commentary I could not stomach the Israeli attitude, and would have been bound to fall out with them.

I should emphasise that I am in no way anti-Semitic. I recognise the appalling sufferings of the European Jews throughout history, culminating in the horrors of Hitler's extermination camps. But I would point out that they had been living in many European and other countries without persecution, and that in modern times at least they were citizens of countries where they had opportunities to prosper of which they took the fullest advantage.

It is also worth remembering that during the mandate they were actively fighting the British and the Arabs by exactly the same methods the Palestinians are using today in order to try and take over a country which their people or many of them had left the best part of 2,000 years before. If we accept the basic premise of Zionism, which is that they have a right to return to Judaea, what about the demands of the Celts to take over Eastern Britain or even their lands around Thracia? The principle is the same.

Terrorism is an appalling feature of 20th century life but if we British had lost the 1939–45 war and become a German colony would we not be applauding our own young men who would be trying in every way they could to dislodge the conqueror and go on doing so for decades or even centuries? Nationalism is almost impossible to eradicate.

Anyway, the first Jews to return to Palestine, as it was then called, were basically idealists who found opportunities of fulfilment while the country was under Turkish rule. They were largely Russian and East European Jews who went there to found centres of communal living on the farms or kibbutzim they set up. The aim of Zionism, a national home, made little headway until the First Great War.

Then in order to get the support of world Jewry the British Government issued the famous Balfour Declaration which promised the Jews a homeland in Palestine alongside the peoples already there. Until the rise of Hitler Palestine was fairly quiet but his persecution caused a vast increase in Jewish immigration. Fearing they would be swamped, the Arabs revolted and fought both the Jews and the British, who held the mandate under the League of Nations.

After the war, in which many Jews fought in the British Army, gaining very valuable training, the refugees, survivors of Hitler's extermination camps, became a flood. This the British tried to stop in the interests of the Arabs and the Balfour Declaration. So the Jews attacked the British until, in 1948, the United Nations devised a scheme of partition and allowed the British to withdraw. After this withdrawal the neighbouring Arab countries attempted to wipe out the Jews but failed. After much savage fighting the State of Israel was formed and still exists. Still growing in population and still at the time of writing attempting to take more land.

No one should underrate the Israelis' achievements. They have succeeded in building a modern European state in the most unpromising surroundings. The land is semi-desert, water is very short, and there are few resources. Their agriculture is first class but by world standards uneconomic. They have urbanised vast stretches of desert. Beersheba, once a desert oasis, now has more than 100,000 inhabitants, Eilat on the Red Sea 20,000.

But none of this would have been possible without enduring aid from countries like Germany with consciences for past misdeeds, or the gifts of rich Jews in many Western countries, plus direct American aid. These donors don't want to come and live in Israel, where conditions are even now insecure and fairly basic, but they like the idea of subscribing to a national home, rather as various Christian churches are supported by their own adherents as a form of conscience money.

Eilat on the Red Sea, Israel.

Refreshment in the Negev desert, Israel.

Avdat in Negev desert. The plots are grown on water retained in sand – a 5,000 year old technique.

Packing lettuces on a kibutz near Beersheba, Israel.

Within these parameters Israel is a most interesting example of a state built on ideology rather than economics. The kibbutz system is, in its extreme form, an example of communal living in which everything is pooled. Once elected, new members donate all their possessions to the kibbutz, and in return are looked after till the grave. Originally based on farming, many have diversified into other trades as their membership increased beyond that which could be employed in agriculture.

But kibbutzim do have other functions. A study of them shows that many have been sited so that frontiers could be defended. Some of them grew up from settlements, originally made by soldiers of both sexes. Kibbutz members are the hard core of Zionism and provide a major proportion of the elite of the fighting services. The disciplines of communal living are not for everyone, so in the other major farming organisation, the Moshav, really a smallholding community, the individuals are allowed more personal freedom. They live in their own houses, for instance, and bring up their own children.

One feature of the kibbutz is the children's section, where all children are reared from an early age. This has its attractions. Fancy having all the fun of children just when you want them, and then handing them over to the professionals when they get difficult. But on one kibbutz I visited the children's committee had issued an ultimatum to certain parents, whose children had got out of hand – 'Make them behave or we quit'. But at another, at a party where the children were watching their elders through the windows long after midnight, I heard one parent demand that the children's committee should see that they went to bed.

Kibbutz life requires great dedication from its members, and a degree of forbearance not granted to many, if the frustrations inseparable from the system are not to get out of hand. Members I met said it wasn't easy, but that the total security offered was by far the best part. This security was instantly apparent in all but the newest kibbutzim I visited, in the calm and unhurried way the members went about their business. No rat races there.

At the time of my last visit I was told that practically all the kibbutzim were heavily in debt, either to the Government or the Jewish Fund. This I can quite understand in view of the unpromising land some of them had to farm and the excess of labour. But as their members provide such a vital part of the armed forces and their sites are in many cases fortresses, these debts are probably considered a good investment.

Some of them are in impossible places. One close to Eilat on the Red Sea boasts the heaviest yielding herd of Friesian type cattle in the world.

There where it hardly ever rains they live under shelters and every ounce of food has to be hauled for them from the Mediterranean coast. The heat is such that even the irrigated production of out-of-season crops in mid-winter is threatened by dehydration.

One or two new military settlements were even more basic with the members still in uniform, learning all about farming and trying to make negligible water supplies go further. Some of these areas on the southern Jordan border and in the Negev desert are beautiful in their differing shades of terracotta and violently jagged hills and mountains. But what a place to farm!

The Israelis were not, of course, the first to live in these parts. At Avdat, south of Beersheba, the Nabateans had a complex farming system in the desert with a 4 in rainfall. The land is undulating with many sand-filled valleys or wadis. In this particular place the Nabateans had, 3,000 years ago, collected the surface stones on the slopes into heaps so that when the rain came, mostly in one or two storms, the water should run off into the sands of the wadi.

The Hebrew University had rebuilt one of these sites and the water stored in the sand was growing quite reasonable crops as the sand prevented evaporation. I asked if the heaping of the surface stones had any significance but was told that they had tried it experimentally, without any discernible difference in collection. Security was a problem here too. The experimental station was surrounded by wire entanglements to which about a dozen dogs were tied. They made such a row that I had a job to do my spiel in front of the camera.

An uncle of mine who had fought in Palestine in the First World War told me that he was once camped on the shores of the Sea of Galilee or Lake Tiberias as it is called now. His colonel was very religious and late one night he heard a great splashing and on looking out of his tent saw the colonel soaking wet wading back ashore saying, 'I don't believe he did it, I don't believe he did it'.

The Sea of Galilee is some 300 ft below sea level, and forms the main source of the country's water supply. It is probably the most productive stretch of water in the world for fish. While filming we took a motor boat out on the lake and could see literally millions of fish lying side by side basking on the surface. The naturally rich water is fed by draining from the farmlands through which the Jordan runs. The source of the Jordan, or Banias as it is called in its upper reaches, is exactly as a biblical spring should be. It wells up out of a rock on the slopes of Mount Hebron, just as if Moses had struck it with his staff. There were some nice small trout in the spring and some quite good ones in the headwaters, but lower down it is too slow and often too salt for worthwhile fish to live.

The Jordan eventually reaches the Dead Sea 1,000 ft below sea level and there evaporates, leaving the salt and minerals behind. I bullied Ronie and John Kenyon to spend a free day seeing if the tales that no human body could sink in it were true. Quite a lot of Israelis had the same idea and we had to change in some fairly sordid sheds. It was far from pleasant, though the water was clear enough. It had a horrid greasy feel on the skin, and when we were swimming it tasted awful.

It was certainly buoyant. So much so that it was difficult to swim without rolling over. It was possible to float in a sort of sitting position, and the pictures I had seen of my uncle sitting reading his paper on it were obviously not faked. Once out it was essential to have a fresh water shower. What would have happened without this was demonstrated by my bathing trunks which I did not wash. They dried out as hard as plywood and started to crack. It is very easy to see how the pillar of salt tale started.

In case you query my statements on the country's economy, just take a look at the trade figures. They make it impossible for the State of Israel to become viable unless they can discover oil or minerals in short supply or marvellous manufacturing processes. Palestine in the old days had one viable export – citrus fruit. Jaffa oranges were famous many years ago. The Israelis grow them well now and have branched out into many other out-of-season fruits and flowers. But the scope for this is limited by land and water resources and the cost of transport to markets, as against exports from Southern Italy or North Africa which make them fairly uncompetitive.

I feel the problem could well get worse. The recession won't go away and the enlargement of the Common Market will bring in competitive areas in Greece, Spain and Portugal which will have preferential access to European markets. Most Israelis don't recognise this, but feel the world owes them a living because of past suffering. And through the adoption of the Hebrew language the bulk of the population are going to understand less and less of the way the rest of the world sees them.

Until the State of Israel was established Hebrew was a scholar's language. Now it is the language of the country and among the younger people nothing else is spoken or even understood. I believe this is catastrophic. It means they are increasingly isolated from what the rest of the world thinks. Perhaps we are mistaken in thinking of them as anything other than a Semitic tribe without European ties or understanding.

21. Dr Malthus and Feeding the Millions

Dr Malthus, a most gloomy cleric born some 200 years ago, has made successive generations' flesh creep. He prophesied that the world would find itself incapable of growing enough food to avoid starvation for the great mass of its people and would end in chaos and disaster. Since his day the world's population has multiplied many times, yet there is still enough food for those who can buy or steal it. I am certain that there are sufficient resources to feed double or even treble the present population of four billion. In fact, from time to time far more food can be grown than the market can absorb. I first saw this in the Argentine many years ago, when the deepening world depression was putting farmers out of business. There were just no markets for what they were growing.

The estancia where I was working was on the main stock route from the south, towards the sub-tropical area along the River Parana. For weeks wagon trains of bankrupt farmers with their horses, domestic animals and families were trekking through to land the government had promised them near the river. It was a custom that the estancia should assist these people with grazing and meat in moderation. They had no money so there was little point in trying to sell them these services. If we had not helped them they would have stolen what they needed. I often talked to them and found they were of Russian extraction, and had been settled some 20 years before in a dry area in the south-west. They had been driven out by a combination of drought and bad prices.

This is worth remembering. As long as prices had been viable they had been able to farm rotationally, and so conserve moisture and a reasonable production. As prices fell away they tried to increase their cash cropping, but yields fell in a declining cycle of bad farming. Exactly the same sequence caused the abandonment of Oklahoma and other states in the dust bowl area of the US, the wheat belts of Australia, and even the arable lands of England. Today the US dust bowl areas are being farmed satisfactorily because governments since the Depression have guaranteed prices. Even then to maintain them land had to be put in the soil bank or 'set aside' as it is now termed. After the Second World War governments of Western countries have with few exceptions taken care to see that their farming survived, by subsidy or other means.

It makes many people very angry to know that there is still hunger in the world while elsewhere farmers are being paid not to produce at all, or penalised if they exceed quotas that have been laid down. Much of this anger is directed at those who are engaged in these restrictive practices. I agree that such systems would be called immoral in a perfect world. But this one most certainly is not. Some say that the richer developed countries have a duty to feed the less developed. Farmers would support this, of course. They would like nothing better than to keep on producing food on a cost plus system ad infinitum. Food to be sent overseas at the taxpayers' expense, making a virtue of an unnecessary exercise.

The fact is that all the problem countries of the world I know about include within their borders enough resources of their own to sustain the lives and health of their inhabitants. That they don't is due to their rulers. Sometimes for various reasons they use their resources to buy armaments or airlines as prestige symbols, or simply syphon their countries' wealth into Swiss bank accounts. But this is no reason for the developed countries to supply them with food ad infinitum.

The trouble is that efficient food production demands money and an intelligent application of known skills. Both these are largely absent from the countries most at risk from hunger. There are always national catastrophes, but these could be coped with as they arise out of comparatively small stockpiles. A reserve of, say, 20 million tonnes of wheat and rice would be no more than 1 per cent of the total world annual production of cereals. It is true, of course, that in the industrialised West farming is highly dependent on factories and finance. This is because the production of unmechanised man is too small to return him a living comparable with that to be earned in the towns. But it need not always be so.

In China, the most thickly populated nation on earth, 11 people are fed and clothed with the produce from one hectare of arable land. It is true that the standard of living does not compare with that in the West. But in China you see no beggars or ragged, or obviously hungry people – common in many countries with many times the area of land per inhabitant to draw upon. The Chinese achieve this with good rotational farming, mostly handwork, and discipline, reinforced by the knowledge that unless they do the job right, they will starve. I thought the rulers of countries always rattling their begging bowls for aid, should be forced to send their farming leaders to China, to learn how to feed themselves. This has nothing to do with Communism, except that this ideology provides the discipline. Knowledge of farming seems inherent in the Chinese character. It is no accident that they monopolise market gardening in many countries to which they have emigrated. But there is no reason why others should not copy them.

Every resource in China is fully used. Most of the communes I visited employed one, two or three people to the hectare. The ripening wheat is interplanted with the cotton or soya for the next crop. Sometimes three crops are taken in 12 months. Human sewage is collected everywhere, even in the centre of Peking, made into compost, and applied by hand round the individual plants. Other fertilisers are used where available, and ammonia factories are built alongside the small coalmines, which seem to be plentiful. I consider what the Chinese have done in feeding a huge population on very little a fantastic achievement.

One of the major factors in increasing food production since the last war has been the development of what are called miracle wheats and rice, the basis of the Green Revolution. I have been privileged to meet Dr Norman Borlaug, one of its originators, and seen his work in Mexico. He is one of that very rare breed, a practical, as opposed to an academic, scientist. He was engaged by the Rockefeller Foundation to go to Mexico and develop a wheat which would yield well in sub-tropical conditions and be able to stand irrigation and heavy applications of nitrogen fertiliser. He did this, not by breeding an entirely new variety from basic genes, but by adapting existing dwarf wheats by a process of selection.

He succeeded admirably. Within 20 years Mexico became self-sufficient in wheat – his first remit, despite a doubling of the population. These strains were taken up across the world, and in no country that I have seen them growing, have they done anything but improve yields. Indian wheat production, for instance, doubled within a very short time. The Chinese have taken them up, as have the Israelis – all under a great variety of systems. This is an important point. The Green Revolution has been attacked most viciously on the grounds that the system requires the industrialisation of farming and the provision of irrigation machinery and nitrogen. It is true that these aids are needed for the best results. But there is incontestable evidence that even when used without these things, they will yield better than existing varieties.

It is also true that without them the world could not possibly have sustained its recent population growth. Those who condemn them should make clear what the alternatives are. I have seen some of them. In the Ivory Coast I visited an inland village just at the moment when the Chief was holding a council to allocate land for the next two or three years' cropping. The village owned a biggish acreage of savannah – grass and scrub. Every two or three years a proportion was set aside for cropping with maize and other crops, grown on individual plots. After a short time yields fall, weeds take over, and cropping moves on to the next patch, leaving the soil fallow until it is needed again. This recovery through the fallow years is well known. I used it myself in the Depression on the arable land on my own farm.

It works in countries like the Ivory Coast where there are five acres of land for every man, woman and child. No matter how badly the farming is done, there will be sufficient to feed the sparse population. But the Ivory Coast is fortunate in its sufficiency of land. Other countries are in trouble because health services have arrived to prevent people from dying from the common tropical ills and consequently life expectancy has lengthened enormously, putting a burden on the land. Then there is education. This has stimulated knowledge of the outside world, the towns and the appetites that these arouse for everything from clothes to Coca Cola. People are no longer going to be satisfied with life under primitive conditions, enjoying primitive resources. So instead of a self-sufficient society, these primitive rural areas are entering a commercial one, at its simplest exchanging their surpluses for spending money.

Once the rural dwellers reach this stage of development, they enter the commercial rat race which engulfs us all. You can deplore it as much as you like, but it is impossible to condemn whole peoples to a primitive rural existence, by denying them the opportunity to emulate the more developed inhabitants of the world. What Malthus should have added, though as far as I know he did not, was that man does not live by bread alone. I have seen some remarkable examples of bringing modern methods and commercialism to farming, which have then been matched by a wholesale flight to the towns. Expectations have been raised, the people have become dissatisfied with what they have got and so they create urban slums.

Dr Norman Borlaug was very well aware of this. While naturally proud of what he and his team had been doing, he always emphasised that his work has done no more than give the world a breathing space, during which the far more difficult job of social engineering, of organising a modern industrial society, could be evolved. Or, if such a society is impossible to achieve, of finding some other way before the world is completely destroyed by universal anarchy. In this I feel we have been badly let down by the United Nations and the Food and Agriculture Organisation, which has cried wolf on food shortages for so long that it is no longer taken seriously. Its spokesmen, led by Lord Boyd Orr, have concentrated on food just as narrow-mindedly as Malthus ever did, and collectively they have been just as wrong. But we do have a responsibility.

The surroundings of the port of San Pedro on the Ivory Coast are at first glance idyllic. The South Atlantic swell breaks against sandy beaches fringed with palms. Dugout canoes shoot the narrow entrance to the harbour, their crews paddling in unison under the shouted orders of their coxwains. The beaches and the harbour are backed by the deep green of tropical forests which hide the scars of modern development. One ship is tied up at the wharves and others are anchored off shore. They are loading logs, great butts of mahogany. I counted 120 lorries, each with its quota of timber waiting to unload. The logs are dumped on the quayside, then bulldozed into the water and chained together in rafts to be towed out to the waiting ships. Assembling the rafts is the work of naked swimmers, Africans who slip in and out between the jostling logs with an apparent disregard for safety.

The port has been built to exploit the natural timber production of the high rainfall tropics. A mahogany tree can develop a five or six foot butt in 70 years. At present they are taking the natural increase, but before long they will be planting this and other trees as a crop. Already they have stands of eucalyptus and tropical pine which can reach a height of 30 ft within three years – ideal material for pulp production when compared with the abysmally slow growth of temperate forests. At the time of my visit there were plans to build a tourist complex here. The sandy beaches were safer than those further south, though communications with the capital, Abidjan, and the international airport were not easy. Anyway a start had been made on building the resort hotel.

But a mile or so behind the beaches, the port and the hotel, was an urban slum of terrifying proportions. Some 36,000 Africans were living in makeshift shacks with one water tap to a terrace, and for the most part absolutely nothing to do. The French, who control the Ivory Coast with a most effective exploitative presence, are very good at what might be called mass hygiene. They had seen to it that there was no disease, but there was certainly evidence of almost every other human ill from starvation to prostitution. Apart from the control of the water supply and the spraying against malarial mosquitoes there was little or nothing in the way of medical facilities. The only doctor allocated to the town had gone to France on leave and had not returned.

I was told that the settlement was illegal, that every effort was being made to keep away the people who flocked to it and try to induce them to return to their villages in the interior. But people were still flocking in, travelling down in the timber lorries or by any other means. They were looking for work and trying to join a money economy. But there was no work to be had. Apart from a few hundreds needed in the port and to service the new resort building there was absolutely nothing. They could not even grow their own food, as the land around was forest and reserved for trees.

The problem basically was that by exporting the trees in the round for conversion in Europe and the United States, the Ivory Coast had simply no opportunity to add value and employment to this trade. I have no idea how much conversion into sawn timber would add in the way of employment, but it is bound to be substantial. To carry the process further and manufacture furniture, pulp and paper products would add still more. But no. To do so would add to the unemployment figures in the developed countries, already reeling under the impact of the mass production of consumer items from the Far East and elsewhere. Unless there is a change of heart and investment policy, it is very unlikely that anyone will build such facilities in the Ivory Coast or places like them. Nor is government aid likely from the West because Western governments with scarce resources prefer to aid their own problem areas. The developing countries have no votes outside their own boundaries.

But development is not always as beneficial to those being developed as would appear. Swaziland is a fortunate place, a small country the size of Wales with a population of around half a million. There is plenty of room for everyone. In 1958 the Commonwealth Development Corporation started a pilot sugar growing scheme in the country. The area chosen was extremely well suited to the crop, fairly low lying with water available and the land readily turned from scrub to cropping. The first settlers were smallholders, and they made a splendid job of it under the guidance of a nucleus of expatriate officers. It is a disciplined operation and leaves little room for individual initiative.

When Britain joined the EEC, production from this scheme and from various private investments had risen to a total of about 100,000 tonnes of raw sugar annually. In accordance with the terms of entry which Britain negotiated for her ex-colonies and protectorates, Swaziland was awarded a quota of 120,000 tonnes. This was under the Lomé Convention, guaranteeing a market in the EEC for 1.2m tonnes of cane sugar mainly to the UK. Other interests then moved in and increased the country's output to more than 200,000 tonnes. Under the rules set out by the Swaziland Sugar Association sales are pooled. While a proportion was sold at the Lomé guaranteed price the balance had to be sold at the world price which in 1979 was about half that figure. This effectively reduced the income per tonne of the smallholders somewhat.

Towards the end of 1979 I was shown a further development which would raise the total output to some 300,000 tonnes. One could not criticise the efficiency with which this latest scheme had been set up. The mill and its surrounding land would be completely integrated and mechanised and employ many fewer people than the smaller smallholding system. In fact, I was told the employment per acre would be no more than would be needed in sugar beet growing in Europe, or cane in Australia. The cost had been very high indeed – some £80 million supplied by Swaziland and a great many other capitalist interests. The whole project shone with efficiency, but again it was staffed by expatriate workers right down to a very low level.

I was told that the Swazis lacked the education to tackle the responsible jobs. They hoped to train them up, but meanwhile every executive job appeared to be going to a non-Swazi. With this in mind, I asked the Minister of Trade and Industry if he thought the expatriates were exploiting the Swazis in this and some other industries. 'Socialistically, no', he said, 'but capitalistically, yes.' A most interesting reply. It is absolutely true that the sugar development, and others for pineapples and forestry, did bring trade and a measure of prosperity to the country, but it seemed to me it was a form of exploitation. The eventual profits would have to be sent out of the country, not only to repay the investment, but to pay the expatriates at work and their pensions too.

There is no doubt at all that the Swazi sugar industry is very well run. That undoubtedly quite a lot of prosperity might spin off on the rest of the community there. It is also true that the world price of sugar has doubled to around the EEC price as I write this in February 1980, and the anxiety about the Lomé Convention quota being disowned in the near future has disappeared. But sugar has a very volatile price pattern and for most of the last 25 years the world price has been running well below the cost of production. One reason for this has been the EEC. Beet sugar production has increased to the extent of producing a surplus of two to three million tonnes annually.

To get rid of this the Common Agricultural Policy has provided export subsidies which must undercut the world price. This has the effect of reducing the world price and in consequence limiting the outlets worldwide of the other sugar-producing countries, or even of local producers. In Chile, for instance, there was a local beet sugar industry. Under the laisser-faire policies of the Chicago economists who have been running the country since Allende was killed, sugar was imported at the going world price. This caused the collapse of the beet industry and even worse unemployment in the rural sector.

Australian interests would have been justified in thinking they could supply sugar to a country as close to them as New Guinea. But they soon found that aggressive EEC salesmen had been dumping European sugar there. To my mind this makes an utter nonsense of any aid programme the developed countries propose. The irony of it is that on the one hand you have governments and charities wringing our hearts and our pockets to provide aid, while at the same time they deny these unfortunates the means of pulling themselves up by their own bootstraps.

It is not only in sugar that the pressures lie. Every one of the developing countries is seeking to improve material standards. Their peoples are not satisfied with a simple diet alone, mere sustenance which there would be no problem in providing within almost every country using modern techniques. In fact, except at times of disaster, every country that I have seen has within its borders the resources to feed itself. Malthus was abundantly wrong. But far worse dangers are upon us. The more you relieve the pangs of hunger, the more time people have to brood about their prospects.

22. The Sugar Crops of Mauritius and Swaziland

One cool December Friday a voice on the telephone asked if I would be prepared to fly to Mauritius and Swaziland the following Wednesday. I said I could not leave my wife lamenting in the gloom of a December week while I went to the tropics. But if she could come, I would be glad to go. I then asked the purpose of the visit. It appeared that the cane sugar refiners, Tate and Lyle, were worried that the supplies they relied on to keep their factories working would be reduced or even wiped out altogether by the Common Market's action to amend the Lomé Convention. This convention guaranteed the developing countries, mainly the ex-British colonies, a quota of imports into the EEC at the guaranteed EEC price for sugar.

At that time the world price of sugar was well below the EEC level, so the advantages of the arrangement were obvious. The worry for the sponsors of my trip was that the Lomé Agreement was rather loosely worded and could be interpreted as limiting the period of the concession. Should the agreement be attenuated or even terminated, the effects on the developing countries, several of which depended on sugar, could be disastrous if world prices remained in their chronically volatile state. It was thought that if I and other responsible journalists were able to publicise the facts, their cause could be furthered. Frankly I don't believe that any amount of sober analysis by journalists, responsible or otherwise, makes much impression on the politicians who decide these things. But the fact that many people do believe this has led me into some extraordinarily interesting places.

The programme was for a flight to Mauritius, three nights there, then three in Swaziland and back home by the following Thursday. A bit rushed, but beggars can't be choosers. I find that once I get going on an excursion of this sort, I just keep going until I fall asleep. I sleep easily, sometimes with my eyes open, so I can be construed as being more alert than I am. Fortunately on this trip every long flight was followed by film depicting the history and achievements of the country visited, so I was able to close my eyes for 20 minutes or so without appearing rude. There was an unexpected bonus. We reached Khartoum where the plane broke down, so we were moved to a hotel, rather a nice one overlooking the Nile. After twelve hours' flying I headed straight for bed, but I had reckoned without Graham Rose of the *Sunday Times*. No sooner was my head on the pillow than he was on the phone. 'I know this place. I worked here after the war, and I have hired a car to have a look round.'

We saw the junction of the White and the Blue Nile, both of the same muddy colour. Then the place where General Gordon was murdered, the Mahdi's tomb and the Souk, or market, of Omdurman. Our visit coincided with the deposing of the Shah of Iran by the Ayatollah Khomeini and other Islamic zealots. The Mahdi had been another of the same calibre, who led the revolution in the Sudan for many years until an army under Lord Kitchener on behalf of the Egyptian Government of the day, defeated him at Omdurman. Winston Churchill was in this battle. Like most British children of my day, I had been brought up to execrate the Mahdi and all his works as opponents of the Pax Britannica. Yet in the hotel I found a brief description of the Mahdi's life and times, coupled with the assertion that this was the most glorious period of Sudanese history.

The Souk was most interesting, with vegetables and local silverware alongside the latest transistors from Japan, enormous cartons of East German glassware, bright tin trays, everything you could think of. The Sudanese are the blackest of all Africans, and their loose white clothing accentuates their magnificent physique. Unlike many African markets the Souk is a man's world, possibly because of the Mohammedan influence. I have been in such crowded places in many parts of the world, and they are often overpowering with a sense of hostility to Europeans or, when this is not present, a definite menace of crime, pickpocketing or thuggery. Here, though dwarfed by the enormous Sudanese, I did not feel any apprehension at all. The Sudan is a Left-wing, almost Marxist dictatorship. The cars and the boats on the river were of very ancient vintage, and most of the buildings unpainted and drab. It was very much like most Left-wing countries I have visited, but the people seemed to have a decided dynamism which probably enabled them to survive in spite of their government.

The next day we flew on over Kilimanjaro, Tanzania and Madagascar –

a huge island where, before the War, I knew a number of penniless young men who had worked on the enormous cattle ranches in some pretty foul conditions. The island used to be French. Remembering the tales those men had brought back of almost incredible hardships, it seemed a good place to cross in less than an hour.

As the plane was losing height, coming into Mauritius, I noticed that, though the country was generally green with the growing sugar cane, in almost every field, there were black dots which grew larger as we approached. 'What are they?' asked Ronie. I could say no more than that I thought they must be residues of old crops. I was wrong. On closer acquaintance these were seen to be piles of rock, often many feet high, which had been removed from the fields to make room for the sugar. When the island was discovered in the 16th century much of the surface was covered with a layer of solid volcanic rock about a foot thick. Over the years this has been painfully removed, mostly by hand, to uncover the soil beneath. This soil is not easy to work. It is still very stony and abrasive, and there is little scope for mechanisation.

There is little chance of diversification either, because sugar cane is almost the only viable crop. The island is subject to cyclones, and no other form of crop could stand up to them. In fact, a few days after our visit a cyclone devastated part of the island, and killed a number of people. Sugar cane is also almost unique among crops in being able to produce an excess of energy, while it is being processed. The bagasse, or waste of the cane, not only powers the mills, but can supply the national grid as well. In Mauritius sugar generally yields fairly well and could yield better if they could find cheap sources of energy for pumping irrigation water. There are no other resources on the island to speak of, beyond a million people who are a mixture of Europeans and natives from most countries bordering the Indian Ocean.

Sugar production amounts to about half a million tonnes on average, which means that each person benefits from the earnings of about half a tonne of sugar, at the Lomé price. This is the importance of the agreement, because without it the sugar earnings at world prices would have been only about 60 per cent of what they have been. Sugar costs here are probably a good deal higher than in many parts of the world. People I met spoke enviously of the French island of Réunion not far away, also dependent on sugar, but with the advantage of being classed as part of Metropolitan France. 'They never lack for schools and roads over there', I was told. Others said it was a pity that Britain took them over after the Napoleonic wars. We should have given them back. Socially and politically there are great tensions. The population is rising, emigration has almost halted, and even the industries into which diversification was attempted have been badly affected by the world recession and by protectionism in Europe and the USA. In addition, the long distances from markets and sources of raw materials are a severe constaint.

We stayed a couple of nights in a lovely tourist spot, Trou-au-Biches – holiday cabins in a coconut grove by the side of a lagoon inside a coral reef. The food was wonderful as long as they stuck to the native seafood. European style cooking was not so good. But I can never believe tourism could possibly become a serious industry so far from the centres tourists come from, especially now the world recession has multiplied travel costs. You have to realise that the Mauritians are all descendants of immigrants to the island. There were no natives here, and they are not people given to sitting in the sun like the South Sea islanders. It is an active, intelligent and very frustrated population. A beautiful but very sad place, I thought.

Swaziland, by contrast, seemed a pleasant place. A country the size of Wales with a population of about half a million, completely landlocked and ruled by a royal family basically controlled by the King's most important wife. South Africa is a close neighbour, but there is no colour bar – in fact no bar to anything. For a long time the fleshpots of casinos and brothels, close to Mbane, the capital, offered the South Africans a safety valve where they could get relief from the austerities of their own country. I was told that the very tight control of speed limits on South African roads, with on-the-spot fines of up to 500 rand, had reduced this tourist traffic.

Most of the land belongs to the state, that is the King. He and his family are involved with a good deal of the development which is going on. Africans, often his relations, are on the boards of many of these companies. Judging by those I met, none of them were passengers. I met some very impressive Africans. One was the Minister of Trade, one of the King's sons. When I asked him if he thought that many European interests which were developing the country were exploiting them, he replied that they were not doing so in a socialist way, but were in a capitalist way. The sugar industry was certainly a capitalist enterprise. It was originally started by the Commonwealth Development Corporation as well as some expatriate farmers and has developed enormously. The CDC began with smallholdings ranging from 15 to 60 acres. The latest was a company, a consortium of many interests, which was breaking new ground and building a completely new factory.

In some respects the sugar was filling an agricultural vacuum. A great deal of the land on which the sugar is being grown had been scrub, carrying no more than a few animals, but was easily cleared and had plenty of irrigation potential. I thought the land was the easiest to clear I had seen anywhere in the world and there were miles and miles of it. There is no land hunger. Anyone who wants a stretch on which to build his kraal can ask his King for it. I was interested to see that most of the workers on the sugar estates in responsible positions were Europeans or Mauritians. The Swazi, I was told, does not like regular work. In fact some of the workers were sent by the local chiefs as a punishment for wrong doing and were apt to clear off as soon as their sentences had been worked out. They did not bother to wait for their wages.

I was taken to the CDC and met one of the largest of the farmers – physically and in terms of land holding. She was a widow, a schoolmistress, whose husband had taken a 60 acre smallholding before he died, which she was carrying on. She spoke very good English, so I asked her what she thought of the new factory that was going up almost within sight of her own farm. She was worried, she told me, that the effect of adding this new factory output to the existing pool would lead to an excess over the Lomé quota allotted to Swaziland, and if the world price were much lower than the Lomé one, their returns would be reduced. What did I think? 'It looks logical', was all I could reply. I had exactly the same response from a ten-acre smallholder I met later.

This CDC scheme, like others I have come across, still depended on considerable control of the tenants by a central authority. It is a practical form of development but does not really inculcate in the tenants the benefits of individual farming. It also depends to a very large extent on expatriate expertise and, of course, on viable world markets for single output enterprises. I met one of the men who had started the newest scheme and asked why he thought the risks were worth it. At that time the sugar market was in a state of depression. Every minute, he told me, more people are being born in the Third World. They are all developing a fondness for sweet drinks, notably Coca Cola. Every week a million more bottles of the stuff are being consumed. There will not be enough sugar to put into them, so the demand will always be there. I was duly sceptical as I had heard similar hopes for other commodities before.

But for a short time I was wrong. The sugar market took off until it far exceeded the Lomé level and for a short time the Lomé countries began to wish they had not signed up at the then price level. Then the inevitable happened. The Americans began to make a sweetener out of maize called

Iso glucose, and one of the soft drink makers said it would be used in their products. The sugar price fell back well below the Lomé line, and looks like staying there. But I felt Swaziland was a happier place than Mauritius. They have all their resources in a large country with a small population. With proper management they will never starve. But having an absolute monarch they might seek political freedom. It is their right, certainly, but will they be any happier?